JavaScript
glossary on demand

a mini guide to modern JavaScript programming
through common terminology explanation

© 2016 **Andrea Giammarchi**
@WebReflection

to the vibrant JavaScript community

Contents

audience: who is this book for ... 13

how to read this book

special thanks

technical editor

the author

what this book is about ... 14

what this book is not

debug ... 15

comments

operators

parenthesis ... 16

brackets ... 17

references

variables

constants ... 18

types ... 19

invoke ... 20

function declaration VS function expression ... 21

named function expressions ... 22

scope

private and nested scope ... 23

context ... 25

global context

method context	26
invoking a function via call or apply	28
explicit context	
arguments	29
Array and generic collections iteration	30
for loop	31
Incremental ++ operator	33
Array methods	34
array.forEach(callback, context)	
array.map(callback, context) → newArray	35
array.filter(callback, context) → newArray	36
array.some(callback, context) → boolean	
array.every(callback, context) → boolean	37
array.indexOf(value, fromIndex) → number	
prototype and prototypal inheritance	38
genericA.isPrototypeOf(genericB) → boolean	39
Object.prototype	40
object.toString() → string	42
native	43
class	44
constructor	45
instance	47
inheritance	48
the in operator	
for/in loop	49

enumerable	50
object.propertyIsEnumerable(name) → boolean	
object.hasOwnProperty(name) → boolean	51
shared properties	
getters and setters	53
descriptors	55
Object.defineProperty(obj, name, descriptor) → obj	56
try catch finally	58
which descriptor for what	59
common property descriptor	
common class and native method descriptor	60
common defensive method descriptor	
common lazy property descriptor	61
Object.getOwnPropertyDescriptor(obj, name) → desc	62
Object.defineProperties(obj, descriptors) → obj	
delete	
Object.getOwnPropertyNames(obj) → arrayOfAllNames	63
Object.keys(obj) → arrayOfOwnEnumerableNames	
public and public static	64
extends	65
super	66
implements	68
interfaces	
trait and mixin	69
`if else switch` and conditional logic	70

conditional statement	70
ternary operator	71
switch statement	72
logical || operator (read as OR)	73
logical && operator (read as AND)	
truthy and falsy values	74
antipattern	
DOM	75
tree	
Web IDL	76
EventTarget registration interface	77
void	
DOMString	78
EventListener	
EventListener using a function	79
function bind	81
Event	83
browser events	
bubbling and capturing	
event.stopPropagation()	85
event.preventDefault()	86
CustomEvent	
EventEmitter	87
signature	88
parameters	

node.js events	89
WeakMap	
Symbol	91
primitives	
Object.getOwnPropertySymbols(obj) → arrayOfSymbols	92
shared Symbols	
special Symbols	93
`for/of` loop	
fat arrow	94
generator	
yield	95
generator.next(value) → {done:boolean, value:any}	97
generator.throw(error)	98
Promises	
promise.then(resolved, rejected) → newPromise	100
promise.then(resolved).catch(anyError) → newPromise	101
promise.then(fn).then(fn).then(fn) → newPromise	
Promise.all(arrayOfPromises) → newPromise	102
Promise.resolve(value) → newPromise	
Generators and Promises	103
Timers	105
setTimeout(fn, delay, arg1, arg2, argN) → timerIdentifier	
clearTimeout(timerIidentifier)	106
setInterval(fn, delay, arg1, arg2, argN) → timerIdentifier	
clearInterval(timerIdentifier)	107

requestAnimationFrame(fn) → rafIdentifier	107
process.nextTick(fn)	108
requestIdleCallback(fn, waitExpiresIn) → ricIdentifier	
template strings	
tagged template strings	109
regular expression	110
JSON	111
Math	
parseInt(string, base) → integerNumber	112
parseFloat(string) → floatNumber	
Recent ECMAScript features	113
`let` declaration	
rest parameters	114
spread operator	
Map	114
Set, and WeakSet	
Proxy	115
destructuring	
JavaScript F.A.Q. on demand	116
Useful links	

audience: who is this book for

For absolute beginners or more advanced developers, this book explains the most common terms used in JavaScript programming, client or server, through examples.

If you cannot understand technical articles, this book will explain each term.

If you are looking to refresh and update your knowledge about modern terminology, patterns, and their applications, this book will also help you.

how to read this book

This book could somehow be compared to a waterfall: it starts quietly, by describing simple basic terms, and then accelerates until it covers most modern features towards the end.

Being a compact book I recommend you do a quick read-through first, and once completed, go back to any specific words, so that every term is clear.

special thanks

To every person that believed in me and helped me with this idea.

In particular: Robert Woloschanowski, Stoyan Stefanov, Arianna De Mario, Cinzia Giammarchi, Maria Teresa Sardella, Luca Vavassori, every member of the TC39 and the ECMAScript Mailing List who in all these years has been patient enough to deal with my questions and rants.

technical editor

A special thanks goes to Stoyan Stefanov, who is the author of JavaScript Patterns, Web Performance Daybook Volume 2, JavaScript for PHP Developers and others O'REILLY best sellers, helped me reviewing content as well as code and examples.

the author

Andrea Giammarchi is an experienced Web and Mobile Development consultant, formerly a Senior Software Engineer at Twitter, previously at Facebook, NOKIA, and others.

what this book is about

Many online articles, as well as many other books, take for granted that the reader knows the meaning of every single term used to describe generic software related topics.

The truth is that there are many people that would like to understand *"what the heck"* is all this programming about, the same people that might stop reading the article, or feel confused, the very moment they come across terms such as `variable`, `reference`, `context`, `scope`, `object`, and so on. While I can instantly assure everyone that programming is not always trivial, and it's surely not something you can possibly learn overnight, or maybe just reading a couple of books, I also strongly believe one really shouldn't need a degree in Computer Science to understand basic articles that, for example, simply use some JavaScript to click a button to show an `alert` ...

... and *"what is an alert?"* It's a modal window with a warning message and an OK button.

... and *"what does modal mean?"* It means it blocks the interaction with the program.

Do you see how many questions already? And the more we describe, the more we understand, the more other terms come up, needing more answers and more explanations.

Well, this is why I've written this *"JavaScript glossary on demand"*, hoping that you won't feel disoriented ever again while reading online articles, or other more advanced books.

what this book is not

Every single term in this book could require a book of its own to describe all its glory, history, or *"gotchas"*. JavaScript (JS) has been around for more than 20 years now, and while I've tried to keep things as simple as possible, the aim is to explain modern JS first, since it's daily JS that you want to learn, and not the one from the 90's.

My apologies in advance if some descriptions are not absolutely perfect. You are the one in charge of any deeper investigation if needed.

So ... shall we?

debug

It's the basis, because it's what we need whenever we write code and we want to know if such code succeeded or failed. This verification procedure is known as *"debugging"*, for the simple reason that it's usually performed through a *"debugger"*, which is a developer's helper tool that most modern browsers provide.

Just try to *"right click"* on any webpage, and see if there is *"inspect element"* as the last option of the menu. This is how you can test all examples in this book: click *"inspect element"* and then the button or tab called*"console"*, and start writing in it pieces of code, also known as *"snippets"*, while we walk through the examples.

As an alternative, you could also use the *node.js command line interface*, since most examples are environment agnostic, which means these will work in every browsers as well as servers.

Every code example contains some grayed out comments, I strongly suggest you read all of them at least once, and focus on the actual programming afterwards.

comments

In programming, comments are meaningful descriptions of the code itself. They are ignored during code execution, and can be

```
// single line
```

ending when a new line is encountered, or

```
/* multi
   line */
```

operators

If you take a calculator, you can see numbers and arithmetic operations on it. In programming it's basically the same, there are arithmetic, comparison, assignment, conditional and other operations. We can use them right away in any console.

```
// let's do some math
1 + 2;   // shows 3
3 * 5;   // shows 15
1 - 2;   // shows -1
```

While in a calculator the sign = means *"show the result"*, in JavaScript it means *"assign the result"*. You can use the = sign to hold some results to be reused later on.

```
var result = 3 * 7;
result; // shows 21
```

If you want to compare two different values, you can use the triple equal operator ===

```
2 === 2;   // true → of course, same number
           // 2 is identical to itself
2 === 3;   // false → well, 2 is different from 3
           // so these cannot be the same
```

To verify that two values are different, you can use the *"not"* version.

```
2 !== 2;   // false → 2 is 2 so it cannot be different
2 !== 3;   // true → of course 2 is different from 3
```

The ! *"not"* operator can be used to negate some logical condition, by inverting its value. For instance, !true === false and vice-versa. If you want to state that different values are in fact the same, you can use logical operators.

```
(4 + 5) === (5 + 4) && (2 * 3) === (3 * 2);
// true → commutative property
```

There is an entire section about these operations further in the book so let's keep focusing on terminology for now.

parenthesis

It is possible to group different sequences of operations via parenthesis. These become instantly more readable, making the developer's intent clear. As an example, if one read an operation such as 2 * 3 + 4 one would think that the result is 10. Instead, you actually meant to multiply the sum of 3 and 4 by 2, and to make it clear to both your eyes and the JavaScript program interpreter, you should write 2 * (3 + 4), which drops all doubts about the result.

Often referenced as *parens* for short, parenthesis are also used as part of functions syntax, which is described later on.

brackets

In JavaScript there are curly brackets {}, or *braces* for short, and square brackets []. These can be used to create objects and, in the square brackets case, also to access their values.

```
// generic reference to an object
var obj = {hello: 'world'};

// generic reference to an Array object
var arr = ['a', 'b', 'c'];

arr[0];      // shows the letter 'a'
obj.hello;   // "world"
//      ↑ could be accessed via obj['hello'] too
```

references

A reference is like a symbolic link that points to a specific value. Think of a selfie, the photo can be considered as a reference to a generic person: you don't need to have this person present in the room to see what she looks like or what she is doing, the photo is enough.

variables

A variable is usually a meaningful name used to reference a generic value.

Back to the example of the selfie, `var myPhoto = new Selfie();` creates a reference to my selfie whose name is `myPhoto`. I can keep it for me, send it around as a postcard, receive other selfies from other people, and reassign its value at any time.

```
// create a variable that references my selfie
var myAvatar = new Selfie();

// ... 5 years later ...

// save the old picture
// by using a new variable name
var oldMe = myAvatar;

// then shoot a new selfie
// simply reassigning it to the same variable
myAvatar = new Selfie();
```

A common JavaScript convention for variable names is
`var camelCase = anyValue;` starting always with the lower case, and eventually putting together multiple words through uppercase letters.

If the composite variable name contains single characters or acronyms in it, it is OK to put together multiple uppercase letters.

```
// common naming conventions examples
var thisIsAGoodNameForAVariable = anyValue;
var result = loadSDK();
object.genericProperty = genericValue;
```

constants

A constant is like a variable but can only be created, and assigned, once. In modern JavaScript engines, it can be explicitly created through the keyword `const`.

```
// instead of var MY_CONSTANT = 'staticValue';
const MY_CONSTANT = 'staticValue';

// it does not change its value
MY_CONSTANT = 'nope';

MY_CONSTANT; // shows "staticValue"
```

Their common naming convention in most popular programming languages is the following:

`EVERYTHING_IN_UPPER_CASE_WITH_UNDERSCORE_BETWEEN_WORDS`

These kind of variables are frequently, but not exclusively, used to describe data which do not ever change and have a fixed value (usually well known), such as the force of gravity or the temperature at which water boils (see the example below).

```
if (room.temperature >=
    WATER_TEMPERATURE_RIGHT_BEFORE_STEAM) {
  console.log('too hot');
} else if (room.temperature <=
        WATER_TEMPERATURE_RIGHT_BEFORE_ICE) {
  console.log('too cold');
}
```

types

When a variable that references a value is created, it can be assumed that this value has a type.

Back to the `var myPhoto = new Selfie();` example, you could say that the type of the variable `myPhoto` would be "*photo*", which describes more or less what one can do with it: look at it, share it, trash it, draw creepy things on top of it via some photo editor, etc.

In JavaScript the "*photo*" type doesn't exist, but there are few others you can consider.

To obtain the type of a generic reference you can write:

```
typeof myReferencedVar
```

boolean represented by two possible values: `true` and `false`.

number represented by integers such as `0`, `1`, `2`, `-3` or floats like `0.9`, `1.2`, `-11.7` and a few special cases such as `Infinity` and `NaN`, which means "*Not a Number*".

How could a number be considered not a number? Think about the result of `0/0`

string represented by anything within single or double quotes: `'I am a string'` and `"so am I"` are indeed both valid strings. Most modern JavaScript engines support also backtick enclosed strings such as `` `this one` ``, which is also a string but with some "*special power*" explained later on.

undefined represented by the absence of a value. By default, there is a global reference to such absence named `undefined`. Its absent value is the exact equivalent of a variable declaration that does not reference to any value:

```
var noValYet;
console.log(noValYet === undefined);   // shows true
```

Please bear in mind that JavaScript has a value that explicitly represents nothing. Such value is actually a reserved, constant-like, keyword named `null`.

The `null` value is also the implicit root of every JS object and its type is "*object*".

object represented mostly by curly `{}` or square `[]` brackets. Objects are containers for *key/value* pairs (also described as properties where each key would be a property name and each value would be a property value). When it comes to square brackets `[]`, the object can also be called *array* and its property names are commonly represented by integer indexes (indices).

```
// create two variables, one Object and one Array
var obj = {aKey: 'a value', bKey: 123};
var arr = ['some value', 456];

typeof obj === 'object';   // true
typeof arr === 'object';   // true

// read an Object property
console.log(obj.aKey);     // 'a value'

// read an Array element by its index
console.log(arr[0]);       // 'some value'
```

function represented by `function name(a,b) { return; }` syntax, or in modern engines by `()=>{}`. Functions are special objects that can be *"invoked"*.

symbol only in modern JS engines, it can be used as special *"object"* property.

invoke

In JavaScript, this term is related to a specific operation: executing any sort of function reference using parenthesis:

```
// declaring a function
function tellMeSomething() {
   console.log('something');
}

// tellMeSomething is the reference name
// of the function we have just declared
tellMeSomething;   // nothing happens
                   // (just shows the function itself)

// to "execute" this function
// we need to invoke it using parenthesis
tellMeSomething(); // logs 'something'
```

If you look carefully, you can see that even the operation `console.log('something');` is invoking a function. However, in such a case the `log` function is invoked through a `console` object reference instead of directly, and it's accessed using a *"dot notation"*.

Every time a function is invoked after a dot, that function can be considered a *"method"*.

function declaration VS function expression

There are a few ways to define a function and each might be more or less convenient.

A function declaration, for example, creates a reference available everywhere within the *"scope"* it has been declared, even if invoked before.

```
// invoke it even before it's declared
readyJack();   // works as expected

function readyJack() {
   console.log('I was born ready');
}
```

This can help you organize code in separate blocks. But it can also be confusing if there are many declarations in various different parts. Since it's a good practice to declare all needed variables together, function expressions might be a better fit.

```
var name = 'Jack';
// function expression referenced via readyJack var
var readyJack = function () {
   console.log(name + ' was just an expression');
};
```

Just like every single variable declaration should end with a semicolon, when assigned to a variable function, expressions should also end with a semicolon.

Semicolons are not needed when it comes to function declarations, as shown in the previous example.

Remember: function expressions cannot be executed before they are defined.

named function expressions

To simplify our own debugging, it's a good practice to give functions a name, even if there is a function expression and a reference to it.

```
var anonymous = function () {};
var named = function helloThere() {};
console.log(anonymous.name);  // empty string
console.log(named.name);      // logs 'helloThere'
```

It must be said that modern debuggers are smart enough to tell the reference name anyway, but it's good to know that you can create function expressions with a name at runtime.

This is particularly handy when you want to immediately invoke the function itself, procedure also known as *IIFE: Immediately Invoked Function Expression*

```
(function areWeThereYet(tenSteps) {
  if (tenSteps === 0) {
    console.log('finally arrived');
  } else {
    console.log('yet another step');
    // use the function name to invoke itself
    // passing the decreased count
    areWeThereYet(tenSteps - 1);
  }
}(10));  // the count in this case starts at 10
```

scope

This term indicates the boundaries in which the code is executed. Think of it as the Universe is every galaxy's scope, the Milky Way is our solar system's scope, the solar system is planet Earth's scope, planet Earth is all continents' scope, and for each continent we are going to have countries, regions, cities, councils and finally your own house, which is your own scope while you are inside it, while the rest of the city will be your scope when you get out.

In JavaScript, by default there is a global scope in which you can define functions and variables.

However, back to the house metaphor, you don't want each neighbor to know about every single thing you do in your place: your home is your place, and functions, in JavaScript, are the way to define your very own place without interfering, or being disturbed, by everything that happens in the middle of the street, or anywhere else, including other houses.

```
// global scope starts before JS code is executed
// (it's already there)
// function `myHouse` scope starts here
function myHouse(sco, ped, args) {
  // defining a variable inside `myHouse`
  // makes it available only here
  var myMess = 'my own room';
} // function `myHouse` scope ends here

typeof myHouse;  // is the 'function' `myHouse`
typeof myMess;   // is 'undefined'
                 // because it's unknown in this scope
```

private and nested scope

Since it is possible to create functions inside other functions, it is also possible to have a private scope within a function that is already private, like a room within the house.

To create a private scope, we can use the previously seen *IIFE* approach without naming our function expression.

```
// anonymous IIFE
(function () {
  var myPrivateScope = 'a string value';
  console.log(typeof myPrivateScope); // 'string'
}());
console.log(typeof myPrivateScope);    // 'undefined'
```

By having an anonymous function expression that invokes itself, you can be absolutely sure that nobody outside that function can be able to interfere with your code.

Moreover, you can define other functions in it, and create nested scopes.

23

```javascript
(function () {
  var who = 'I am ';
  var nestedExpression = function () {
    // nested function expression scope
    var nested = who + 'expression';
    return nested;
  };
  function nestedDeclaration() {
    // nested function declaration scope
    var nested = who + 'declaration';
    return nested;
  }
  console.log(
    nestedExpression(), // 'I am expression'
    nestedDeclaration() // 'I am declaration'
  );
}());
```

It is important to remember that nested scopes can always access their outer scope variables or references but never vice-versa.

This is why it is possible, for both function expression and declaration in the previous example, to use the who reference while executing.

However, it wouldn't be possible for the private outer scope to reach the nested variable defined inside each nested function: these are reachable only via their own function scope.

The reason we want to use private scopes when defining our own variables, and the reason we create functions at all, is to prevent conflicts with any other variable name that could possibly be already present in our application.

It is also a way to automatically clean up or free memory once we have completed the task the function is supposed to solve.

context

Every time a function is invoked, it is possible to reference its current execution context through the automatically available `this` reference, which has one of the following values:

- the global program context, called `window` in browsers and `global` on server
- the generic `obj` object that invoked the function through the dot notation: `obj.method()`
- an arbitrary explicit value, including `undefined`, when invoked via function methods like `.call` or `.apply`

global context

If you open your browser console, or start node js, you can inspect the global context writing `console.log(this);` or simply `this`.

Whenever you define a variable or declare a function globally, you are also able to reference these variables through the global context, since it is just like an object.

```
// create a variable directly in the global scope
var globallyDefinedVar = 'can everyone access me?';
// it's accessible through the global object
console.log(this.globallyDefinedVar);

// the same when you create a function
function globallyDeclaredFunction() {
   return globallyDefinedVar;
}
console.log(globallyDeclaredFunction());
```

It is also possible to define global variables inside a generic function by accident, by simply omitting the `var` keyword before assigning a value to a reference.

```
console.log(typeof a);   // 'undefined'
function myScope() {
   a = 123;              // instead of var a = 123;
}
myScope();
console.log(typeof a);   // 'number'
console.log(a);          // 123
```

To prevent accidental global scope and context pollution, the 5th version of the ECMAScript specification (the standard that defines JavaScript semantics, syntax and behavior) introduces a special `"use strict"`; directive.

This string, if placed at the beginning of a function, will guard the global context and switch into a more strict behavior. If you try the previous code again, you will see an Error instead of the number 123.

```
console.log(typeof a);    // 'undefined'
function myScope() {
  'use strict'; // switch local scope to strict mode
    a = 123;
}
myScope();                // shows an Error
console.log(typeof a);    // still 'undefined'
```

Not only it's impossible to define variables in the global scope by accident, but when this directive is used, the execution context will also be `undefined`, unless explicitly provided.

```
// defined in the global scope
function whoIsThis() {'use strict'; return this;}
whoIsThis();          // undefined
this.whoIsThis();     // the global context
```

method context

In JavaScript objects can have properties of any kind and functions are no exception.

```
// create an empty object
var obj = {};
// define a property as function expression
obj.somePropertyName = function () {
   return this;
};
// what would be that returned context value?
// let's figure it out invoking obj.somePropertyName
obj.somePropertyName(); // exactly the obj itself
```

When a function is invoked through an object, it implicitly uses this object as its current execution context.

It is important to remember that any function can be attached to any object at any time, even if it is not directly defined as a property of that object.

```javascript
// generic function defined here or somewhere else
function sayTheName() { console.log(this.name); }
// generic object
var me = {};
// with a name property and 'Andrea' as value
me.name = 'Andrea';

// function sayTheName attached as 'whoAmI' property
me.whoAmI = sayTheName;

// so we can invoke it as method
me.whoAmI(); // 'Andrea'
```

Even though it is not such a good idea to attach methods at runtime, the fact that we can borrow functions of any kind and use them as methods in different objects is nonetheless an amazing feature. *"Why would we need that"* is more than a legit question, and the answer is that, for example, each collection of items does not necessarily have all methods like a regular Array. Online it is indeed possible to find some code examples similar to the following:

```javascript
// COUNTEREXAMPLE
var allNodes = document.querySelectorAll('*');
// borrow the forEach method from an empty Array
allNodes.forEach = [].forEach;
// iterate over all nodes using the method
allNodes.forEach(function (node) {
    console.log(node.nodeName);
});
```

As already mentioned, modifying objects one didn't create is a very dirty approach, even if it is possible. As an example, if we take someone for a ride in our shiny new car, we don't want them to leave food crumbs and dirt all around. It wasn't there when they got in, why should it be now!

Good news: there are better and cleaner ways to invoke a function by providing a context.

invoking a function via call or apply

As described in the *types* paragraph, functions are special objects that can be executed. Just like any object, functions can also have properties, hence methods. The most commonly used methods of any function are `.call()` and `.apply()`, which only differ in that while `.call` accepts an arbitrary amount of arguments to pass along, `.apply` accepts only an array to be used as invocation arguments.

```
// three functions that log some information
function fnWithNoArguments() {
  console.log('nothing to do here');
}
function fnWithOneArgument(first) {
  console.log('received', first);
}
function fnWithTwoArguments(a, b) {
  console.log('received', a, b);
}
// using call ignoring for now the `context` value
fnWithNoArguments.call(null);
fnWithOneArgument.call(null, 'some value');
fnWithTwoArguments.call(
  null, 'first value', 'second value'
);

// to use `apply`, you need one or more Arrays
var emptyArray = [];
var arrayWithOneArgument = ['any value'];
var arrayWithTwoArguments = ['1st', '2nd'];

// same result as you logged already via .call
fnWithNoArguments.apply(null, emptyArray);
fnWithOneArgument.apply(null, arrayWithOneArgument);
fnWithTwoArguments.apply(null, arrayWithTwoArguments);
```

Tip to remember the difference between `.call` and `.apply`: the word *"apply"* starts with *"a"*, and so does `array` ;-)

explicit context

Now that the difference between these two methods is clear, it's time to understand what's powerful about them.

Do you remember the collection in the previous page?

```
var allNodes = document.querySelectorAll('*');
// a dirty and not always possible approach
// allNodes.forEach = [].forEach;

// this is one way to borrow and invoke
// the Array forEach method
[].forEach.call(allNodes, function (node) {
  console.log(node.nodeName);
});
```

🔧 Invoke the following function through its `.call` method passing, as first context argument, any sort of value that will be returned as this.

```
function whoIsIt() {'use strict'; return this;}
whoIsIt.call(null);
whoIsIt.call(123);
whoIsIt.call(['a', 'b', 'c']);
```

arguments

Every time a function is invoked, it might receive from zero to many arguments, each of which is also the name of the special object that gets created each time a function is executed.

```
function contextAndThreeArguments(a, b, c) {
  console.log(this, a, b, c);
}
var me = {name: 'Andrea'};
contextAndThreeArguments.call(me, 1, 2, 3);
```

Not only the object me will be the execution context, you'll also log in the console three different arguments: 1, 2, and 3. The fact that you have named your arguments a, b, and c, means that you expect a maximum of 3 of them and no more. But what if you don't know upfront how many arguments you expect?

```
// no specific amount of args expected
function contextAndArguments() {
  console.log(this, arguments);
}
var me = {name: 'Andrea'};
contextAndArguments.call(me, 1, 2, 3);
contextAndArguments.call(me, 4);
contextAndArguments.call(me, 5, 6, 7, 8, 9, 10);
```

The output in the console will be quite different this time.

You will see a list of values enclosed in square brackets such as [1, 2, 3] and [4] or [5, 6, 7, 8, 9, 10], which represent the collection of items the current `arguments` object contains for each different function execution.

Please note that `arguments` is not actually an `Array`, even if its structure looks similar: you access its properties using integers and it has a `length` property.

```
function argumentsVSArray() {
  // almost every object has a toString method
  // it usually describes what kind of object
  // you are dealing with
  console.log(arguments.toString());
  // you create a collection of 3 elements
  var arr = [
    arguments[0],   // arguments value at property 0
    arguments[1],   // arguments value at property 1
    arguments[2]    // arguments value at property 2
  ];
  // Array has a special toString method
  // that joins all elements instead
  console.log(arr.toString());
}

argumentsVSArray('a', 'b', 'c');
```

As `arguments` is not an `Array`, you see the string `'[object Arguments]'` instead of `['a','b','c']`.

In this example you access all indexes manually, but what if there were more than 3 arguments?

Array and generic collections iteration

When talking about iteration we describe the process that accesses every property, hence every value, of a generic object.

If we are dealing with an Array or a generic list, such process is represented by a loop that accesses every index between 0, and the length of the collection itself, which is available through the special property `.length`

```javascript
var list = ['a', 'b', 'c'];
var index = 0;
var sizeOfTheGenericList = list.length;
// a while loop executes what's inside
// its curly brackets until a condition is satisfied
// while (condition) {
//    do something and update the condition
// }
// in this case the condition is:
// "the `index` is less than `sizeOfTheGenericList`"
while (index < sizeOfTheGenericList) {
  console.log(list[index]);
  // update the index so that we can
  // get out of the while loop whenever index is
  // no longer less than `sizeOfTheGenericList`
  index = index + 1;
}
```

The very first time the condition is satisfied, the index variable has the value 0 which is less than the `sizeOfTheGenericList`, whose value is 3, since there are 3 items in the `list`.

In the console you see the letter `'a'`, then you increment the `index` by 1, and you check the condition again.

At this point `index` has the value 1, which is still less than 3.

Then you need to log the value at `index` 1, which this time shows the letter `'b'` and then you need to do the same again for the `index` 2 and the letter `'c'`.

After that, the condition is no longer satisfied so whatever is inside the loop won't execute anymore.

for loop

Similarly to the previous `while(condition){...}` example, the `for` loop also executes until its condition is no longer satisfied.

However, its logical order is slightly different and described as such:

(please note the following is not valid JavaScript code, just a textual description)

```
for (
   [1] one or more, comma-separated,
       variable declarations;
                              ▲
                              └──────── first semicolon
   [2] condition to satisfy ; ◄──────── second semicolon
   [4] changes to update the condition
) {
   [3] do something with the current value.
       Please note this is actually the third part
       of a for loop flow.
       The 4th part comes after this one
}
```

Taking into consideration the previous `while` loop as an example, you can do exactly the same process within the following `for` loop:

```
for (var index = 0, size = list.length;
         index < size;
         index = index + 1
) {
   console.log(list[index]);
}
```

It is very important to note that if the condition is not satisfied, neither the 3rd nor the 4th part of the `for` loop is executed.

```
// empty list, its length is 0
var list = [];
for (var
   i = 0;
   i < list.length;// the condition is never satisfied
   i = i + 1       // it won't happen if the condition
                   // exited the loop
) {
   console.log(i);
}
console.log(i);    // 0 because the 4th part i = i + 1
                   // never happened
```

As soon as you put at least one item in the list, the condition is satisfied (at least once) and you'll see that the value of `i` after the loop is 1 instead of 0.

incremental ++ operator

It is very common to increment integers using a ++ sign instead of reassigning the variable to itself adding 1. Accordingly, the following example is how a `for` loop usually looks like:

```
for (var i = 0; i < collection.length; i++) {
    // do something with collection[i];
}
```

The ++ operator can be used both before or after a variable. In both cases the variable is incremented, but its immediately returned value is quite different.

```
// using ++ as suffix (a.k.a. post-increment)
var num = 0;
var numPlusPlus = num++;
console.log(numPlusPlus);  // 0, when assigned,
                           // num wasn't incremented yet
console.log(num);          // 1, because after num++
                           // it got incremented

// using ++ as prefix (a.k.a. pre-increment)
var num = 0;
var plusPlusNum = ++num;
console.log(plusPlusNum);  // 1, when assigned,
                           // num was already incremented
console.log(num);          // 1, ++num incremented num
                           // and returned it as 1
```

There is no specific reason to prefer one way or the other, and while num++ is usually preferred, ++num could also be used as an example to loop over a collection with at least 2 items:

```
var i = 0;
while (++i < list.length) {
   compare(list[i-1], list[i]);
}
```

Decreasing an integer by 1 (decrementing) is also possible using the -- operator, simulating the operation num = num - 1.

Everything already mentioned for the ++ operator, including the differences when used as prefix or as suffix, equally applies for the -- decremental operator.

Array methods

In JavaScript, every array comes with some special methods, used to change, copy, update, or iterate its items. Not only methods look somehow cleaner than loops, but it's common to borrow them to iterate over any sort of collection, arguments included.

array.forEach(callback, context)

This is probably the most *"as close as possible to a loop"* arrays' method, and it works like this:

```
['a', 'b', 'c'].forEach(
  function (value, index, array) {
    // the function will be called array.length times
    // in the ['a', 'b', 'c'] list case means 3 times
    console.log(index, value);
    //              0,     'a'
    //              1,     'b'
    //              2,     'c'
  }
);
```

The anonymous function is invoked three times, receiving those arguments by default.

Let's reconstruct what happens in a `forEach` using the good old loop syntax.

```
for (var
  list = ['a', 'b', 'c'],
  context,    // unless specified,
              // the forEach context is undefined
  callback = function (value, index, array) {
    console.log(index, value);
  },
  i = 0;
  i < list.length;
  i++
) {
  // log same sequence previously logged via forEach
  callback.call(context, list[i], i, list);
}
```

The context is a feature that is rarely used, but very handy in some cases.

As there are collections that might not have a `forEach` method, you can borrow its iteration capability.

```javascript
// the current user on a generic social page
var user = {
  name: 'Andrea',
  // a method to write the user name
  // in a generic DOM element
  writeNameInEl: function (element) {
    // expect `this` to be the user object
    element.textContent = this.name;
  }
};
// find all nodes that should show the user name
var nodes = document.querySelectorAll('.user-name');

// iterate over nodes invoking user.writeNameInEl
// and pass `user` as `forEach` iteration context
[].forEach.call(nodes, user.writeNameInEl, user);
```

array.map(callback, context) → newArray

If instead you want to create a new array based on some value found during the iteration, `.map()` is the right way to go. Its usage is basically the same as for the `forEach` one, but its invoked function should return some value for each iterated index.

```javascript
var single = [1, 2, 3];
var doubled = single.map(function (num, i, arr) {
  // returning a new value for index i
  return num + num;
});

console.log(single);    // [1, 2, 3]
console.log(doubled);   // [2, 4, 6]
```

The main use case for `map` is to create a new list of items after somehow extracting, changing, or transforming the initial values of a collection.

```javascript
var people = [{name: 'Andrea'}, {name: 'Robert'}];
var allNames = people.map(function (obj) {
  return obj.name;
});
console.log(allNames);  // 'Andrea', 'Robert'
```

array.filter(callback, context) → newArray

In case you want to work only with items that satisfy a specific condition, you can use the `filter` method which creates a new array containing only those items that pass the check.

```javascript
var smallerThan10 = [1, 5, 8, 12, 16].filter(
  function (num) {
    return num < 10;
  }
);
console.log(smallerThan10); // [1, 5, 8]
```

One should never confuse the meaning of the returned value in `.map()` with the one returned in `.filter()`, because while the former will use as value for that index whatever value you decide to return, including undefined in case no value is specified, `.filter()` returned value will be just the condition indicating if the value at the current index should be kept or not in the new array.

array.some(callback, context) → boolean

You now know how to iterate, how to transform and how to filter; but how do you look for a specific condition inside a collection?

Well, in this case `.some()` is your best friend as it stops iterating as soon as the returned value satisfies the condition.

```javascript
var people = [{name: 'Andrea'}, {name: 'Robert'}];

function isThereAny(name) {
  return people.some(function (user) {
    // as soon as this is true it will stop iterating
    return user.name === name;
  });
}

console.log(isThereAny('Andrea'));  // true
console.log(isThereAny('Jack'));    // false
```

array.every(callback, context) → boolean

To the contrary of `.some()`, the following method stops iterating as soon as the condition is not satisfied:

```
var people = [
  {name: 'Andrea', age: 37},
  {name: 'Robert', age: 17}
];

function canEveryoneDrink() {
  return people.every(function (person) {
    return person.age >= 18;
  });
}

console.log(canEveryoneDrink());
// false, Robert is too young
```

array.indexOf(value, fromIndex) → number

As its name suggests, `.indexOf` finds the index, if any, that holds a specific value within an array.

```
var alphabet = ['a', 'b', 'c', 'd', '...', 'z'];
var index = alphabet.indexOf('c');  // index === 2
alphabet[index];                    // 'c'

// if not found, returns -1
alphabet.indexOf(123);              // -1
```

In the latest specifications, `array.includes(value, fromIndex)` returns a `boolean` indicating the value is present or not.

There are actually dozens of array methods. All of them are described with many examples and uses in the *Mozilla Developer Network*, under the section *Array.prototype*, which is the object containing all methods and behaviors inherited by every array.

MDN Array.prototype

https://developer.mozilla.org/en/docs/Web/JavaScript/Reference/Global_Objects/Array/prototype

prototype and prototypal inheritance

When a new variable has the value of an object, an array, or a function, it comes by default with methods that nobody explicitly assigned: these are already part of the core functionality; they are properties, and methods, inherited from another object.

There are two mechanisms to inherit from other objects: via direct link or via special functions used to initialize objects and setup their inheritance.

The first direct link way to explicitly inherit properties between objects, is the following:

```
// generic object referenced as a `person`
// it has two properties: `name` and `age`
// and a method in charge of increasing the age
var person = {
  name: 'anonymous',
  age: 0,
  birthday: function () {
    this.age++;
  }
};

// this is just me, inheriting
// properties and methods
// from the `person` object
// using a method of the globally always available
// `Object` "constructor" (described later on)
var me = Object.create(person);
me.name = 'Andrea';
console.log(me);        // {name: 'Andrea'}
console.log(person);    // {name: 'anonymous', age: 0}
```

Usually the browser console will only show objects *"own"* properties, ignoring the inherited ones.

That is why logging the variable me, you see only the name property, even if there's more in there.

genericA.isPrototypeOf(genericB) → boolean

In JavaScript, one of the methods available by default is `.isPrototypeOf()`, which reveals possible inheritance information between two objects.

If you consider the previous variables `person` and `me` as an example, you can assume the result of the `person.isPrototypeOf(me)` invocation will be true.

But what does it mean, exactly?

```
// how does the console show me?
console.log(me);
// {name: 'Andrea'}

// but does me have an `age` too?
me.age;
// 0 → Yes, `age` is inherited from `person`

// and does me have a `birthday` method too?
typeof me.birthday;
// 'function' → Yes, inherited from `person`

// what happens if we invoke the `birthday`
// as method of `me`?
me.birthday();

// how did `birthday` invocation affect me?
console.log(me);
// {name: "Andrea", age: 1}
//    and suddenly,  ▲ "the wild age appears"

// did me birthday affect person one?
console.log(person);
// {name: "anonymous", age: 0} → Nope, all good
```

A little recap of the method context chapter: when we invoke a function through the dot notation from a generic object, that object will temporarily become the execution context of such function.

This does not mean that both `person` and `me` have a `birthday` method, but it means that `me` will temporarily execute `person.birthday` as if it was its own method.

39

```
// `root` is an object with a method that
// simply returns the current execution context
var root = {method: function () {
  return this;
}};

// `child` is an object that inherits from `root`
var child = Object.create(root);

// if you execute `root.method` via `root`
// it will return `root` itself since
// it's the implicit execution context
console.log(root.method() === root);
// true → because `this` is `root` here

// but when you invoke the inherited method
// through the `child` reference it returns
// the current execution context
// which is `child`, not `root`
console.log(child.method() === child);
// true → since `this` is now `child`

// and that is because we are implicitly
// doing the following:
root.method.call(child);
// which will use `child` as `this` indeed
```

Once you understand that a method does not need to be directly attached or assigned as an object property, and that it can be simply inherited, what the prototypal inheritance is about becomes clearer: it is an implicit, *"invisible"*, chain between different objects.

Object.prototype

By default, every JavaScript object inherits properties from the `Object.prototype`, which is also simply an object, in fact the one that provides basic methods to all the others.

```js
var empty = {};    // create an empty object

// can this object be represented as a string?
console.log(empty.toString());// '[object Object]'

// but who put that `toString` method
// into your empty object?
console.log(
  empty.toString === Object.prototype.toString
);                 // true

// is that because there is a prototypal chain
// between these two objects?
console.log(Object.prototype.isPrototypeOf(empty));
// true
```

Since every object has in its root a `.toString()` method, you might think it will behave in the same way, regardless of which variable you use, right? Well, no. Inheriting some property or method doesn't prevent possible *"overrides"*, therefore a method could have been redefined in the middle of some inheritance chain. For instance `Array.prototype` also inherits from `Object.prototype`, and you could always perform an `array.isPrototypeOf(anotherObject)` check. But the `toString` method is not the inherited one. It's redefined to return its comma-separated values that are also *"converted"* into a string.

```js
// create a generic Array containing 3 numbers
var arr = [7, 11, 2];
// the arr.toString method
// is inherited by Array.prototype
// and not by Object.prototype.
// The following check is indeed false
console.log(
  arr.toString === Object.prototype.toString
);                 // false

// but other methods are inherited from the root
console.log(
  arr.isPrototypeOf === Object.prototype.isPrototypeOf
);                 // true

// how different is it?
console.log(arr.toString()); // shows '[7,11,2]'
```

object.toString() → string

Being at the root of the prototypal chain has some advantages.

For instance, even if array inherits a different `toString` method, you can temporarily borrow the method at the root and see how different the result is.

```
var arr = ['a', 'b', 'c', 'd'];
console.log(
  // the inherited method is
  // the one from Array.prototype,
  Array.prototype.toString.call(arr),// 'a,b,c,d'
  // which is indeed the equivalent
  // of the following operation
  arr.toString(),                    // 'a,b,c,d'
  // but Array.prototype inherits
  // from Object.prototype
  // and what happens when you use
  // the original method instead?
  Object.prototype.toString.call(arr)// '[object Array]'
);
```

The `Object.prototype.toString` method is a very special one: it can tell you if you are dealing with some generic object or a *"native"* one.

As in the previous example, using an array as `Object.prototype.toString` execution context will return the string `'[object Array]'`, very differently compared to `'[object Object]'` which is the default string returned for every object in our program.

native

In JavaScript, this term means all variables, objects, functions, methods, classes or constructors that have been provided by the environment and not by a library.

Objects derived from native classes in JavaScript expose their *"class"* name once they are used as context of the `Object.prototype.toString` method.

```js
// being lazy and for demo purposes
// let's reference the method directly
var ts = Object.prototype.toString;

// so that it is possible to easily invoke it multiple times
console.log(
  ts.call({}),              // '[object Object]'
  ts.call([]),              // '[object Array]'
  ts.call(''),              // '[object String]'
  ts.call(0),               // '[object Number]'
  ts.call(true),            // '[object Boolean]'
  ts.call(null),            // '[object Null]'
  ts.call(undefined),       // '[object Undefined]'
  ts.call(function () {}),  // '[object Function]'
  ts.call(JSON),            // '[object JSON]'
  ts.call(Math),            // '[object Math]'
  ts.call(new Date),        // '[object Date]'
  ts.call(
    this.window || global   // '[object global]'
  )
);
```

Historically, unlike many other cases, the `Object.prototype.toString` method has been implemented in a consistent and reliable way across platforms.

class

In most modern JavaScript implementations, `class` is a very specific keyword used to define the behavior of each object that will be created through its name.

Following there is an example of modern JS syntax, which might not work in older browsers or JS engines

```js
// define a generic Rectangle behavior
class Rectangle {
  // this method will implicitly be invoked
  // every time a new Rectangle(w, h) is created
  constructor(width, height) {
    // the `this` invocation context will be
    // the freshly created new object
    // you assign the received arguments
    // to use them later on
    this.width = width;
    this.height = height;

  } // ← note that a class definition
    //   doesn't need a comma between methods

  // the definition includes an `.area()` method
  // that will be inherited by each `new Rectangle`
  area() {
    // the execution context will be
    // the `Rectangle` instance that is invoking
    // the area method. Every instance will have
    // `width` and `height` properties,
    // assigned when created
    return this.width * this.height;
  }
} // note: no comma required here either

// a `Rectangle` instance example
var myDesk = new Rectangle(5, 3);
console.log(myDesk.area()); // 15  as 5 * 3
// another reference
var myTV = new Rectangle(16, 9);
console.log(myTV.area());    // 144
```

Whenever in JavaScript the special keyword `new` is used, the engine expects a class or a *"constructor"* right after `new` in order to create an object linked to the `constructor`'s own `prototype`.

constructor

Whenever you declare a function, the engine will automatically provide its `prototype` object.

```
function aFunction() {
  /* and it could do anything it wants */
}

console.log(
  // who put this object here?
  aFunction.prototype,                             // {}
  // is that inherited from the global Function?
  aFunction.prototype === Function.prototype // false
);
```

Generally speaking, every JavaScript function can be used to create objects linked to their own prototype, which is an object that contains only one property: the constructor

```
function linkMe() {} // simple function

// linkMe becomes special
//the moment we invoke it via new
var obj = new linkMe();

console.log(
  // we have created a prototypal chain
  linkMe.prototype.isPrototypeOf(obj),    // true
  // by default we also have inherited
  // the constructor which is nothing else
  // but the function linkMe
  obj.constructor === linkMe,             // true
  // and such constructor is actually
  // inherited since it is indeed part of
  // linkMe.prototype itself
  linkMe.prototype.constructor === linkMe // true
);
```

Going back to the `Object.create(fromAnotherObject)` mechanism you saw previously, you can use functions to create new instances, as in the following operation:

```
// dummy function used only to inherit its prototype
function Shape() {}

// creating a chain using the Shape.prototype
var oneShape = Object.create(Shape.prototype);

// is the same as creating a new Shape
var anotherShape = new Shape();

console.log(
  Shape.prototype.isPrototypeOf(oneShape),     // true
  Shape.prototype.isPrototypeOf(anotherShape)  // true
);
```

The biggest difference between these two approaches, is that using `new Shape()` inevitably invokes the `Shape` function, implicitly using the fresh newly created instance as an execution context.

That in turn will, for example, give us the ability to do some setup in there.

```
// as a naming convention, classes are
// PascalCase (capital first letter)
function Person(name) {
  this.name = name;
}

var me = new Person('Andrea');  // the class way

// the equivalent procedural and explicit way
var me = Object.create(Person.prototype);
// invoke the Person to setup me.name
// otherwise there won't be any name property at all
Person.call(me, 'Andrea');
```

In either case, the generic object created either via `Person`, or from its prototype, inherits a `constructor` property which is `Person` itself, like it was for the generic function.

To summarize: when we talk about a `constructor` in JavaScript, we refer to the special method that will implicitly initialize any instance as soon as it gets created via the `new` keyword.

instance

Whenever an object is created using `new Constructor`, it can be called an instance of that `Constructor`.

This helps us name expected behaviors as defined by classes, instead of referencing objects as linked to the `prototype` inherited via such `constructor`.

- Q : *"What is myDesk?"*
- A1: *"it's a Rectangle instance"*
- A2: *"it's an object that inherits from Rectangle.prototype"*

As you surely agree, it's more convenient to discuss references by using the term *instance*, and JavaScript has a similar special keyword for that:

```
function Person(name) {
  this.name = name;
}

var rob = new Person('Robert');

console.log(
  Person.prototype.isPrototypeOf(rob),   // true
  rob instanceof Person                  // true
);
```

inheritance

We have already mentioned the prototypal inheritance, but we haven't seen how it works in practice. Here is a basic textual example of the logic behind an object property access.

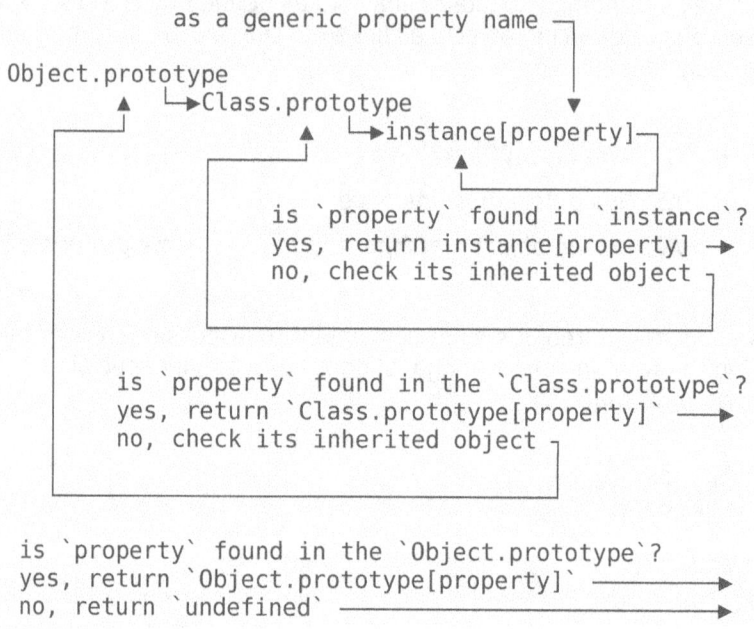

the in operator

If you want to know whether a generic property name is reachable through an object, you can use the `in` operator which inspects any inheritance chain.

```
var obj = {key: 'value'};

console.log(
  // is property 'key' reachable through `obj`?
  'key' in obj,        // true
  // is also 'toString' reachable through `obj`?
  'toString' in obj    // true → via `Object.prototype`
);
```

It is also very important to remember that knowing that an object can access a specific property through its prototypal chain, does not mean that this property contains any value.

As an example, even `undefined` can be considered a property of the global execution context.

```
var root = this.window || global;
console.log(
  // does the global context
  // contain an undefined reference?
  'undefined' in root,   // true
  // does it mean such property has a value?
  root.undefined         // undefined → so, nope!
);
```

This is why it is common to see code online that checks both for property existence and a returned value, assuming that, if defined, it gives access to the expected value or method.

```
// one way to check the existence of properties via
// their "truthy" value
if (obj.hasSomeMethod) {
  obj.hasSomeMethod(some, value);
}
```

for/in loop

Having seen how to loop over arrays indexes, now we surely want to know how to loop over object properties. The `for/in` loop is the traditional way to do it, and here is how:

```
// yet another `me`
var me = {
  twitter: '@WebReflection',
  name: 'Andrea',
  age: 0
};

// loop all key/value pairs and log them
for (var key in obj) {
  console.log(key, obj[key]);
}
// twitter @WebReflection, name Andrea, age 0
```

enumerable

After all the considerations made about the inheritance and the fact that the `in` operator can easily inspect it, it might come as a surprise that the `for/in` loop does not show all properties and methods inherited from the `Object.prototype`.

```
var empty = {};
for(var k in empty) {
  // does not appear in the console
  console.log('why this never happens?');
}
// but this logs `true`
console.log('toString' in empty);
```

First of all, the `in` used to loop via `for/in` has a different meaning compared to `prop in obj`. Also, properties can be or not be enumerable. As a consequence, they might expose themselves in a `for/in` loop, or be simply skipped or ignored.

For example, every native JavaScript constructor such as `Object`, `Array`, `String`, or any other, has properties defined in their `prototype` as non-enumerable.

object.propertyIsEnumerable(name) → boolean

The `Object.prototype` provides a few handy methods and `propertyIsEnumerable` is one of them. It returns `true` if the property has been assigned, or configured as enumerable, otherwise it returns `false`. As already mentioned, native properties aren't enumerable.

```
var obj = {prop: 123};
var root = Object.prototype;
console.log(
  obj.propertyIsEnumerable('prop'),      // true
  obj.propertyIsEnumerable('toString'),  // false
  root.propertyIsEnumerable('toString')  // false
);
```

If you loop over obj with a `for/in` loop, you'll see that `'prop'` is revealed in there, but nothing else is.

object.hasOwnProperty(name) → boolean

How is it possible to tell whether a property (or method) has been inherited or not?

The answer is in the method `hasOwnProperty`, which returns `true` only if the property is an own one, directly attached, not inherited.

```
var obj = {prop: 123};
var root = Object.prototype;
console.log(
  obj.hasOwnproperty('prop'),      // true → defined
  obj.hasOwnproperty('toString'),  // false → inherited
  root.hasOwnproperty('toString')  // true → it's own
);
```

In case you are wondering why you need to know about all those methods, the answer is because prototypal inheritance can be both powerful and dangerous at the same time.

For instance, setting a property like

`obj.toString.prop = 'value';`

will not simply affect the method `toString` of that `obj` reference, instead it will affect the universally inherited `toString` method, because that's what you access whenever you invoke a `generic.toString()` that hasn't been redefined.

shared properties

When talking about classes and prototypes in particular, but also when there is a private scope and some private reference, the term *"shared"* describes the fact that a method, an object, or a function, is used in many different places, for similar purposes, and via many objects.

```
function SharedData() {}
SharedData.prototype.data = {}; // will be inherited

// Note: parenthesis are optional
var one = new SharedData; // two different instances
var two = new SharedData; // that inherit from
                          // SharedData.prototype

one.data.test = 'one check, one check';

console.log(
  // did previous operation affected `two.data`?
  two.data.test,          // 'one check, one check'
  // is that because `one` and `two`
  // are sharing the same data?
  one.data === two.data
  // true → it's exactly the same reference
);
```

The above example is one of the reasons modern JavaScript `class` syntax doesn't allow the definition of properties to be different from that of methods, with the only exception of *"getters"* and *"setters"*, which are special kind of methods with *"implicit invoke"* capability. Back to the shared data issue, whenever we want to setup some data property per each instance, the constructor is surely the best place to do it.

```
function NotSharedData() {
  this.data = {}; // ← the right place to create
                  //   instances own properties
}

var one = new NotSharedData;
var two = new NotSharedData;

one.data.test = 'one check, one check';

console.log(
  // did previous operation affect `two.data`?
  two.data.test,          // undefined
  // is that because `one` and `two`
  // are sharing the same data?
  one.data === two.data
  // false → each instance has a different data
);
```

For comparison sake, in a modern environment the above class would look as follows:

```
class NotSharedData {
  constructor() {
    this.data = {};
  }
}
```

getters and setters

If someone asks *"what time is it?"* we would have to check our watch, our phone, or *"our meridian"* before answering, because we don't keep constant track of time.

Metaphorically speaking, a similar situation happens every time we access the .length property of an array: it will count how many items it has at that moment and will return the count as integer.

Also, in the same way as we can set the time on our watch, we can also set the .length of our array.

But what happens in that case?

```
var arr = ['a', 'b', 'c'];
console.log(arr);           // 'a,b,c'

// it counts its own items and returns 3
console.log(arr.length);
// what if we set the length?
arr.length = 2;

console.log(arr);           // 'a,b' → we lost the index 3
console.log(arr.length);// 2 → so we lost 'c' too

arr.length = 5;             // even re-setting the length
console.log(arr);           // 'a,b' or 'a,b,<3 empty>'
console.log(arr.length);// 5
// and indexes 2,3,4 are undefined
```

Getting or setting the length seems like a transparent operation. However, the truth is that behind the scenes there is definitively something else going on!

If you are familiar with web pages, you might know that there are properties like `el.textContent` or `el.innerHTML` (where `el` is any DOM element) that once modified could visibly affect the entire content of the page.

All these apparently *"magic"* properties and behaviors are possible thanks to getters and setters.

They are not different from a generic method, but you don't need to explicitly invoke them.

```
var me = {                          // hi, it's me again ^_^;

  // basic properties
  name: 'Andrea',
  realAge: 37,

  // and a method to grow up too
  birthday: function () {
    this.realAge++;
    console.log('Happy birthday ' + this.name);
  },

  // getters and setters have a special syntax

  //  - if you ask my age I'll tell you
  get age() { return this.realAge; },

  //  - but if you try to set it…
  set age(newAge) {
    console.warn(
      'I am afraid I cannot change my age to ' + newAge
    );
  }
};

console.log(me.age);       // 37
me.age = 40;               // Warnig: I am afraid
                           // I cannot change my age

me.birthday();             // Happy birthday Andrea
console.log(me.age);       // 38
```

When it comes to modern classes, the syntax is very similar to the one just seen above.

```js
class Person {
  constructor(name, age) {
    this.name = name;
    this.realAge = age;
  }
  birthday() {
    this.realAge++;
    console.log('Happy birthday ' + this.name);
  }
  get age() { return this.realAge; }
  set age(newAge) {
    console.warn(
      'I am afraid I cannot change my age to ' + newAge
    );
  }
}

var me = new Person('Andrea', 37);
console.log(me.age);        // 37
```

However, when using function prototypes, you need to use another utility whose aim is to define properties via an object, also known as a descriptor.

descriptors

In JavaScript, every property of any object could be described through the following characteristics:

- **enumerable**, that is the property is easily discoverable via `for/in` and other cases
- **configurable**, that is the property can be deleted or configured again

Accordingly, if you want to define the property as *accessor*, via getters and setters, or directly as value, handy for data or methods, you can also have the following characteristics:

- **writable**, indicating whether such property can be modified or not
- **value**, indicating the actual value to assign as property

Whenever you need to *access* the property via `get` and `set`, instead of the previous two characteristics you can use the following:

- **get**, which is the method implicitly invoked when a property is accessed
- **set**, which is the method implicitly invoked when a property is assigned

These two kind of descriptors are called *data* descriptor or *accessor* descriptor.

Data		Accessor	
	default		default
enumerable	`false`	enumerable	`false`
configurable	`false`	configurable	`false`
writable	`false`	get	`function () {}`
value	`undefined`	set	`function (value) {}`

It's important to remember that those two kind of descriptors and their different properties are not interchangeable.

When we define `get` or `set` we cannot define the `writable` property, neither the `value`.

The getter function will return the expected value while the setter could update it or even *"throw"* an *Error*, whenever convenient, to explicitly make it non writable.

Object.defineProperty(obj, name, descriptor) → obj

Now that you know pretty much everything about descriptors, it's time to understand how they can be used.

Here is an example of the *"public"* method `Object.defineProperty`:

```
var square = {size: 8};

Object.defineProperty(square, 'area', {
  configurable: true,   // you can delete it later on
  get: function () {
    return this.size *
           this.size;   // it's calculated each time
  },
  set: function () {    // it will not be allowed
    throw new Error(
      'One does not simply change a square area'
    );
  }
});
// read the area
// it invokes the descriptor `get` as method
console.log(square.area); // 64
// change square size
square.size = 4;
// read it again
console.log(square.area); // 16
// try to set the area directly
square.area = 32;            // red errors in console!
```

And how can we create a square that cannot ever change its `size` value?

```
var fixedSquare = Object.defineProperty({}, 'size', {
  // explicitly enumerable to simulate {size: 8}
  enumerable: true,
  // explicitly non writable (false by default)
  writable: false,
  // initial, non writable, size value
  value: 8
});
console.log(fixedSquare.size);    // 8
// even if we try to change its value
fixedSquare.size = 16;
console.log(fixedSquare.size);    // still 8
```

When it comes to properties that shouldn't be writable or configurable, a setter can surely provide a better mechanism to inform the program that something is wrong. Using a data descriptor will indeed fail, but expecting a new property to change its value while it doesn't might lead to unexpected logical results.

try catch finally

Whenever a program is executed, there are many kinds of errors that could happen.

Some errors might be expected, some errors might be fatal. Most known fatal errors in Computers history are the *"guru meditation"* and the *"blue screen of death"* as they appeared in good old Commodore Amiga or Windows Operating Systems.

We definitely don't need to try and replicate a fatal error, especially because we actually hope that it will never occur. What we can do though, is to try and prevent those errors that will interrupt our application and exit without having any idea of what happened.

The `try/catch/finally` statement gives us a way to deal with errors we might expect to happen, a way to also generate *Errors*, expecting somebody else to react accordingly.

```
// checking if a possibly non existant reference
// can be invoked
try {
  iAintEvenDefined();
} catch(errorObject) {
  console.warn(errorObject.message);
}
// note that finally is optional

// creating a property that throws an error
var me = Object.defineProperty({}, 'name', {
  enumerable: true,
  get: function () { return 'Andrea'; },
  set: function () {
    throw new Error('I already have a name');
  } // `throw` is the keyword used
    // to inform the program about an Error
});

console.log(me.name);               // Andrea
try { me.name = 'Robert'; }
catch (whatHappened) { console.warn(whatHappened); }
finally {
  console.log('Hello ' + me.name);  // 'Hello Andrea'
}
```

The excessive use of these mechanisms is rarely a good idea. Having too many `try/catch` statements around, doesn't necessarily mean the code is more secure or immune to errors. On the contrary it might indicate we have no control, or even worst no idea at all, of how many things could possibly go wrong. There are better approaches to control our application, and on top of that, `try/catch` statements might also slow down the execution of the code considerably. As a summary: use this feature carefully, only when necessary, and applying common sense.

🔍 Error objects have a `.message` property which is a *string* containing the info passed when the `new Error("info")` object was created.

which descriptor for what

Having various ways to define a property can be both handy and disorienting. There are so many glitches to talk about when it come to descriptors, but it's best to stick to common conventions available in the JavaScript core.

For instance, every generic object property assignment will be a *writable*, *configurable*, and *enumerable* descriptor, whose *value* would be exactly the one provided.

common property descriptor

```
var me = {name: 'Andrea'};
me.age = 37;
```

Both `name` and `age` properties, will have similar descriptors. Below you can see the `name` descriptor:

```
// representation of the me['name'] property descriptor
({
  configurable: true,
  enumerable: true,
  writable: true,
  value: 'Andrea'
})
```

Whenever you want to set a generic property like `name` or `age`, it really makes little sense to use the tedious `Object.defineProperty` approach.

Specially because all defaults configuration are `false`, not `true`, and there's no need to type that much!

common class and native method descriptor

While data properties, such as a name or an age, are usually those iterated, collected, or manipulated, it is rarely convenient to have methods in our way. Especially when instances are used, where all methods are inherited, you don't really want them to show up in your `for/in` loop. It's not necessary to know that every object will have a toString.

Accordingly, all native methods available in JavaScript can be described as follows:

```
// representation of the native
// Object.prototype['toString'] descriptor
({
  configurable: true,
  // to never show up in for/in loops
  enumerable: false,
  writable: true,
  value: function toString() { [native code] }
})
```

It is actually lucky that native descriptors are configurable and writable, as it means that they can be reassigned and fixed, whenever necessary.

common defensive method descriptor

If we are creating a class for our own purposes, we probably want to ensure that its methods cannot possibly be modified elsewhere, during the application execution.

In these cases we might want to set methods directly in the prototype as follows:

```
// define a property method
// directly in the class or function prototype
Object.defineProperty(Constructor.prototype, 'method', {
  // defaults: enumerable, configurable, writable: false
  // it won't be possible to patch or change this method
  value: function () { /*...*/ }
});
```

common lazy property descriptor

When we talk about lazy properties, we refer to those properties that will have an expected value only after the first time we need them.

Imagine we are going to buy a car.

By default it comes with many features (properties), but we can ask for even more properties.

On paper, the car has a USB port to connect our devices, but it will be configured like that only if we ask for it, not by default.

```
class CarOrder {
  constructor(chosenColor) {
    // color is an own property set
    // during car creation time
    this.color = chosenColor;
  }
  // usbConnector as lazy property
  get usbConnector() {
    // it is configured on demand the first time
    Object.defineProperty(
      this,
      'usbConnector',
      {
        configurable: true,
        value: {usb: 'connected'}
      }
    );
    // returning the new usbConnector
    // will not pass through the class getter
    // because now it is an own property
    return this.usbConnector;
  }
}
```

The reason we need to use `Object.defineProperty` to configure a lazy descriptor is that if we try to set `this.usbConnector = {}` directly, we'll inevitably end up invoking the inherited setter already defined in the `CarOrder` class `prototype`.

Moreover, if we want to be able to change the port in the future, we should grant the possibility to remove this connector or replace it, which is why we've set it as *configurable*.

Object.getOwnPropertyDescriptor(obj, name) → desc

The last important information about descriptors is that not only you can set them, but you can always retrieve them too. Let's try to play around with this method, exploring, or validating everything we've learned so far. Have a closer look at the `Object.prototype`:

```
// used as shortcut
var getOwnDescriptor = function (object, name) {
  return Object.getOwnPropertyDescriptor(object, name);
};
// some inspection of one of
// the most indirectly accessed JavaScript class
console.log(
  getOwnDescriptor(Object, 'prototype'),
  getOwnDescriptor(Object.prototype, 'toString'),
  getOwnDescriptor({name: 'Robert'}, 'name'),
  getOwnDescriptor(this.window || global, 'Object')
);
```

🔧 to better understand descriptors, run above code in console

Object.defineProperties(obj, descriptors) → obj

The plural version of `Object.defineProperty` somehow simplifies the multiple descriptors assignment, as it requires less typing (which is always a plus! ;-))

```
var me = {};
Object.defineProperties(me, {
  name: {enumerable: true,  value: 'Andrea'},
  age:  {enumerable: true,  value: 37}
});
```

delete

When there is a configurable property, not only we can use the `defineProperty` again to change its descriptor, but we can also use `delete` to erase such property from the object.

```
// do you remember? by default all properties
// are defined as configurable
var me = {name: 'Andrea'};
delete me.name;      // true
'name' in me;        // false
console.log(me.name); // undefined
```

The returned boolean value indicates either that there was nothing to do, so the property can eventually be reassigned to that object without problems, or that such property was there but it was removed.

Remember: `delete` returns `false` only when an own property is non configurable and cannot be deleted.

Object.getOwnPropertyNames(obj) → arrayOfAllNames

We have already mentioned `object.hasOwnProperty(propName)`, but how do we actually get all own properties defined directly in a generic object?

```
// maybe I don't want to tell my age to everyone
var me = { name: 'Andrea' };
Object.defineProperties(
  me,
  { age: { writable: true, value: 37 } }
);

for (var k in me) console.log(k, me[k]);
// the above logs the `name` "Andrea" ...
// ... but what about the age?

console.log(Object.getOwnPropertyNames(me));
// ['name', 'age']
```

Once there is a way to retrieve all named properties of an object and their descriptors, we have everything we need to analyze any kind of objects.

Object.keys(obj) → arrayOfOwnEnumerableNames

This *"public"* method is similar to `Object.getOwnPropertyNames` but it returns an array of the object's own enumerable-only properties.

public and public static

We have been using methods such as `Object.keys` among others which are exposed through the globally available `Object` class. There also are other methods, in most of the native classes.

`Array.isArray(obj)`, `String.fromCodePoint(0x1F4A9)`, or `Number.isNaN(0/0)`, just to name a few.

These are methods related to the constructor they are attached to.

It is possible to define similar *"static"* methods ourselves, in the good old way.

```js
function Rectangle(w, h) {
  this.width = w;
  this.height = h;
}

// Remember: functions are just like objects
Rectangle.isSquare = function (instance) {
  return instance.width === instance.height;
};

// let's test two different rectangles
var spongeBob = new Rectangle(2, 3);
spongeBob.pants = new Rectangle(2, 2);

// invoke the Rectangle.isSquare
console.log(
  Rectangle.isSquare(spongeBob),       // false
  Rectangle.isSquare(spongeBob.pants)  // true
);
```

In most updated JavaScript engines, you actually have a special `static` property for that.

```js
class Rectangle {
  static isSquare(instance) {
    return instance.width === instance.height;
  }
  constructor(w, h) {
    this.width = w;
    this.height = h;
  }
}
```

The `Rectangle.isSquare` method has the following characteristics:

- it's not inherited, but it's publicly available via the `Rectangle` constructor
- it's static, that is it is not expected to be used, or being invoked, with an execution context at all. We can even write `Rectangle.isSquare.call(null, spongeBob)` and it still returns `true` if that instance is a square. No `this` context involved whatsoever!

The latter conditions are the same for every public static function.

For instance, `Object.keys` doesn't need the `Object` context in order to be executed, and it's also not inherited.

```
// public static Object.key function shortcut
var keys = Object.keys;
// so that we can directly use it later on
keys({a, 'a'});
```

extends

The inheritance journey started by talking about objects inheriting from other objects.

It ends up now by talking about classes extending other classes.

There is no reason to freak out, it's just the shorter answer to the following question:

- Q : *"What is Square?"*
- A1: *"it's a class that extends Rectangle"*
- A2: *"it's a class whose prototype inherits directly from Rectangle.prototype"*

There is no concrete limit to the amount of prototypes an object can inherit from, but there is only one direct *"extend"*, which in JavaScript is only possible between two classes.

Accordingly, when we use the term *"extend"* we can only refer to a very specific relationship.

```js
// a Rectangle constructor
function Rectangle(w, h) {
  this.width = w;
  this.height = h;
}
// ... with an area getter
Object.defineProperty(Rectangle.prototype, 'area', {
  get: function () {
    return this.width * this.height;
  }
});

// a Square constructor
function Square(size) {
  // invoke the "super" (parent) constructor
  // which will setup our current instance context
  Rectangle.call(this, size, size);
}

// here Square extends Rectangle through its prototype
Square.prototype = Object.create(Rectangle.prototype);
var twoXtwo = new Square(2);
console.log(twoXtwo.area);   // 4 → 'cause 2 * 2 === 4
```

super

Whenever the word super, or sometimes parent, appears in *Object Oriented Programming*, it refers to the closest ancestor class from which the current execution context inherited from.

It is a special keyword that should never be used outside a generic class method. It used to be a reserved word, something that could break a JavaScript application when encountered.

In pre-*ECMAScript2015* era, before the class keyword got promoted from the status of reserved word to the status of one in use, only some libraries were using this keyword as a property to shortcut the access to anything provided from the inherited prototype.

These days thought, it's quite common to see its usage in the wild.

```
// the class Rectangle in ES6 → a.k.a. ES2015
class Rectangle {
  constructor(w, h) {
    this.width = w;
    this.height = h;
  }
  get area() {
    return this.width * this.height;
  }
}

// how we use the `extends` keyword now
class Square extends Rectangle {
  constructor(size) {
    super(size, size);
  }
}

var twoXtwo = new Square(2);
console.log(twoXtwo.area);       // 4
```

Please bear in mind that if you need to call a super method that is not the constructor, you need to access it through the dot notation, for example: super.calculateArea().

In both cases, the super method execution context is automatically recognized, so you don't need to use .call() or .apply(), the new syntax takes care of that.

implements

As I am writing, this term is not actually part of current JavaScript specifications.

It usually indicates that a class, or a generic object, is implementing some interface.

interfaces

An interface is usually a behavior described through methods or properties.

Interfaces can be used to simply describe expectations: they don't need to implement any logic at all.

As an example, the following is a partial Human class described through the amount of interfaces it implements.

> (the following text in not JavaScript but an example of how interfaces look like)

```
interface Walking
  method moveLegs(whichSpeed)

interface Breathing
  method inhale()
  method breatheOut(afterHowLong)

class Human implements Walking, Breathing
```

Remember: the term *"partial"* is also commonly used to describe some application, class, or object, that is not yet fully composed into its final *"shape"*.

trait and mixin

These two terms indicate a similar concept: an object, or function, which is capable of enriching another object, class, or function, bringing its own specific behavior.

```javascript
// basic mixin utility
function mixin(source, target) {
  // per each property name in the target object
  Object.getOwnPropertyNames(target).forEach(
    function (key) {
      // enrich the source object
      // using the same target[key] descriptor
      Object.defineProperty(
        source, key,
        Object.getOwnPropertyDescriptor(target, key)
      );
    }
  );
  return source;
}

// simple trait we can use to enrich any object
// it has the whole logic in it
var circle = {
  r: 0,                    // initial radius value
  get circumference() { // calculate the circumference
    return this.r * 2 * Math.PI;
  },
  get area() {             // calculate the area
    return Math.pow(this.r, 2) * Math.PI;
  }
};
// generic shape, any object would do
var shape = {};

// we just need to enrich the object
// with one or more mixins
mixin(shape, circle);

// now if we have a radius of 12
shape.r = 12;
console.log(              // we'll see
  shape.circumference,    // 75.39822368615503
  shape.area              // 452.3893421169302
);
```

Composing objects, or prototypes, via mixins, doesn't necessarily need to be an alternative to classes, it's actually the opposite.

Enriching prototypes via traits can make our code better organized and extremely portable.

It doesn't matter which class and what's inheriting, you can make it capable of multiple other behaviors as you need.

There probably are many other details you might want to learn regarding *Object Oriented Programming* and JavaScript, but among these pages the majority of words used to describe code snippets, applications, or anything else in regards to objects of any kind, have been covered at least roughly.

if else switch and conditional logic

It might feel weird to start reading about basic boolean logic after a comprehensive introduction to a more complex subject as *Object Oriented Programming* is, but the reason behind it is that at least now you should be able to understand even more complex examples.

conditional statement

Almost all programs are based on conditions. A login is performed only `if` user *and* password are known in the database.

A lift moves to other floors only `if` we press a button *and* nobody passes through its doors `while` they are closing, otherwise it opens the doors and starts the whole procedure over.

A countdown rings `if` its value reached 0 ... and so on.

Everything we do daily, and everything that surrounds us is based on basic `if...else` flows, and the same can be applied to any piece of software that may or may not do something.

The following code is a made up example on how our driving routine is based on conditions.

```
function letsDrive(car, where) {

  // we start the engine only if off
  if (car.isEngineOff()) {
    car.startEngine();
  }

  // let's move carefully in case of rain
  if (global.weather.isRaining()) {
    car.goSlowerThanUsual();
  } else {
    car.goUsualSpeed();
  }

  // how about the radio?
  if (Date.now() < global.today.LATE_MORNING) {
    car.radio.findMorningNews();     // every day
  } else if (where === 'beach') {
    car.radio.findSurfingSongs();    // on vacation
  } else {
    car.radio.findRockNRoll();       // every evening
  }
}

var myNewCar = new Car();
// and every time I need to drive
letsDrive(myNewCar, 'my office');
```

An `if` doesn't always require an `else`, and there could be an optional `else if` in between.

ternary operator

The most used inline `if...else` shortcut is provided by the ternary operator that looks like a question mark: `?`

It does one thing: it returns its first value if the condition is `true` or the second one, if the condition evaluates to `false`.

```
var ternaryResult = (14 / 7 === 2) ?
  'correct' :         // assigned if true
  'back to school!';  // assigned otherwise
```

switch statement

If the ternary operator is a shortcut for an `if...else`, the `switch` statement is the shortcut for a long list of `if...else if...else if...else` conditions.

```javascript
function isLetterInAFRange(letter) {
  var result;
  // switch syntax, pass any value
  switch (letter) {
    // it will be compared for each case like
    // if (letter === 'G') ...
    case 'G':
      // if the comparison is true, it'll execute
      // the following operation
      result = false;
      // you can arbitrary break it,
      // exiting from the switch
      break;
    // or you can create different entry points,
    // also known as "fall-through"
    case 'A':        // else if (letter === 'A')
    case 'B':        // else if (letter === 'B')
    case 'C':        // else if (letter === 'C')
    case 'D':        // else if (letter === 'D')
    case 'E':        // else if (letter === 'E')
    case 'F':        // else if (letter === 'F')
      // all above conditions return true
      result = true;
      break;
    // no condition satisfied?
    // There is a default fallback
    default:
      result = false;
      break;    // optional within the `default` part
  }
  return result;
}
```

The number of `else if (letter === 'A') { ... } else if (letter === 'B') { ... }` would have made your code look like an octopus designed by Picasso.

logical || operator (read as OR)

Instead of many `else...if` that would result in performing the same action you can use `||`.

Accordingly, the previous example can be re-written in the following way:

```
function isLetterInAFRange(letter) {
  if (
    letter === 'A' || letter === 'B' ||
    letter === 'C' || letter === 'D' ||
    letter === 'E' || letter === 'F'
  ) {
      // whenever a function returns,
      return true;   // it exits from it
  }
  // this gives you the ability to avoid a redundant
  // `else` because there's really nothing else to do
  return false;
}
```

logical && operator (read as AND)

On the contrary of the `||` operator, the `&&` operator keeps checking conditions only if the previous one has been validated. This is probably one of the most important concepts to keep in mind.

For instance, the following *ATM* operations will not be executed together, but one at a time.

```
function getMoney() {
  if (
    cardIsValid() &&     // is the card valid? OK ... next
    pinCodeIsValid() && // is the pin known? Next!
    userSelectedAmount()// any selected amount of money?
  ) {
    // OK then, return money
    return getAmountSelectedByUser();
  }
  return 0;              // something went wrong
}
```

It is also possible to combine both operators, somehow simulating what the ternary one can do.

```
// ternary operator via boolean logic
console.log((1 < 2) && 'OK' || 'EPIC FAIL');   // 'OK'

// equivalent of the ternary operator
console.log((1 < 2) ? 'OK' : 'EPIC FAIL');     // 'OK'
```

However, whenever we need a ternary logic we should probably use the appropriate operator.

truthy and falsy values

The `if` or `else...if` statement, as well as ternary or logical operators, are very merciful. It doesn't matter if we check an actual boolean type `true` or `false` value. The value `false`, together with the number `0`, the empty `""` string, the `null` value, the `undefined`, and the exceptional `NaN` references, are considered *"falsy"* values. This means that everything else is considered *"truthy"*, as if it was a true condition.

```
if ({}) console.log('any object is truthy');
if ([]) console.log('even empty arrays');
if (-1) console.log('or negative numbers');
if (function(){}) console.log('or functions');

// falsy values ... all checked, not a single one passes
if (false || NaN || "" || 0 || null || undefined) {
  console.log('this message will never be shown');
}
```

antipattern

Not necessarily related to the boolean logic, the term anti-pattern indicates some bad practice, or some logic with well-known and undesired side effects in our code. For instance, simulating a ternary operator, instead of using it, constitutes an anti-pattern.

```
true ?  console.log('OK') :
        console.log('FAIL');   // 'OK' → correct

true && console.log('OK') ||
        console.log('FAIL');   // 'OK' then 'FAIL'
```

This happens because `console.log` always returns `undefined` which is *"falsy"*!

DOM

The *Document Object Model* refers to *"the parallel world"* represented by any Web page.

It's a huge set of interfaces that describe the capabilities and behaviors of every *HTML* element, *SVG* and *XML* node, or foreign object available through the document tree.

Whenever we deal with an object that comes from a page, we can call it a *DOM Node*.

tree

Many DOM nodes can contain other elements.

The hierarchy is nested, from a universal root node down to every single node, with possible multiple nodes at the same level.

Following there is an example of a simple HTML page and its document tree.

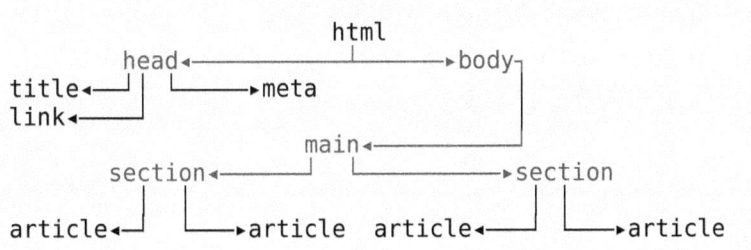

Describing the tree above in JavaScript, you can imagine the following object representation.

```
({ nodeName: 'html',
  children: [
    { nodeName: 'head',
      children: [
        { nodeName: 'title'},
        { nodeName: 'meta'},
        { nodeName: 'link'}
      ]},
    { nodeName: 'body',
      children: [
        { nodeName: 'main',
          children: [
            { nodeName: 'section',
              children: [
                { nodeName: 'article'},
                { nodeName: 'article'}
              ]},
            { nodeName: 'section',
              children: [
                { nodeName: 'article'},
                { nodeName: 'article'}
              ]}
          ]}
      ]}
  ]})
```

It must be said that DOM nodes provide much more than just a `nodeName` or a `children` property, and the best place to read documentation about it is the W3C website.

The entire reference is explained through interfaces, and its written in *Web IDL* format.

Web IDL

It is a dialect used to describe DOM related interfaces, and what matters most to us is to know what an interface's purpose is, and to somehow be able to read what it is expected when using such an interface.

EventTarget registration interface

As an example, if you read the definition of an `EvenTarget` (an interface implemented by almost every DOM node one can think of), you'll find it described as following:

```
// the interface name, if it implements other interfaces
// it will have a colon after the name and what it
implements
interface EventTarget {
  // the returned type + the method or property name
  void              addEventListener(
  //                  in ParameterType + name
                      in DOMString type,
                      in EventListener listener,
                      in boolean useCapture
                    );

  void              removeEventListener(
                      in DOMString type,
                      in EventListener listener,
                      in boolean useCapture
                    );

  boolean           dispatchEvent(in Event evt)
                    raises(EventException);
};
```

The above description basically states that every node will have an `addEventListener('type', listener, false)` method in charge of registering an event and its `removeEventListener` counterpart, plus a `dispatchEvent(event)` method that could eventually raise an `Event` exception.

The documentation provides a more detailed explanation of every single method and the meaning of each accepted parameter, but there are a few new terms here.

It would be good to clarify them as to better understand what we're talking about.

void

The JavaScript equivalent of the `void` term would be `undefined`. It's also a JS historical operator, which is similar to `typeof`, but always returns `undefined` no matter what.

```
console.log(void 0);           // 0 or any other value,
                               // always logs undefined
console.log(void "hello");     // undefined
```

DOMString

Not much different from a generic JavaScript string. Nothing new to learn for once.

EventListener

The *W3C* documentation is great because whenever there is an interface you don't know, there usually also is a link where the interface is described. Regardless, we can easily say that the `EventListener` is probably the most misunderstood interface on the web. Let's see how it has been described via Web IDL in the year 2000.

```
interface EventListener {
    void              handleEvent(in Event evt);
};
```

Whenever an event is registered, we can pass an object with a `handleEvent` method. Below there is an example code that works via a browser console. Once you write everything in there, all you have to do is to click anywhere on that page, except on links.

```
var listener = {
    // if there is a handleEvent method,
    // it will be invoked when the event occurs
    handleEvent: function (event) {
        // where was this listener registered?
        var node = event.currentTarget;
        // is this listener the document indeed?
        console.log(node === document);     // true
        console.log(this === listener);     // true
        // let's clean up by removing this listener
        // the event.type is always available, it is
        // the string used to register the listener
        node.removeEventListener(event.type, this);
    }
};
// register the listener, it should log once if we click
document.addEventListener('click', listener);
```

A `handleEvent` method can also be inherited through a `class`, confining the logic within each instance.

```
function ClickCounter(el) {
  // we register the click for this element
  el.addEventListener('click', this);
  // we also register a way to eventually drop it
  el.addEventListener(this.drop, this);
}

ClickCounter.prototype = {
  drop: 'drop:click-counter',  // custom event type
  value: 0,                     // where the count starts
  handleEvent: function (evt) {
    var el = evt.currentTarget;
    if (evt.type === this.drop) {
      // remove the listener
      el.removeEventListener(evt.type, this);
    } else {
      // show the count
      el.textContent = ++this.value;
    }
  }
};

// here is a new ClickCounter instance
// that shows clicks on the body
new ClickCounter(document.body);
```

EventListener using a function

The reason this interface is considered the most misunderstood is that almost everyone uses functions, instead of objects, to register events.

"Why is that?" Back in 2000 when developers were trying to make events work in both standard and non standard browsers, there was no easy way to replicate the object behavior via ugly `attachEvent` and `detachEvent` non standard alternatives.

The fallback to *"functions only"* somehow compromised old books, articles, libraries, and frameworks, introducing problems that were already solved with the standard interface.

```javascript
// same logic as seen before, using a function
document.addEventListener('click', function (event) {
  // where was this listener registered?
  var node = event.currentTarget;
  // is this listener the document indeed?
  console.log(node === document); // true
  console.log(this === document); // true again
  // if we don't name our function listener
  // we won't ever be able to remove it
  // because we don't have a reference, i.e.
  // node.removeEventListener(event.type, ??what??);
});
```

Whenever we use a function as the event listener we automatically opt in for the following:

- the `this` execution context always points to the `event.currentTarget` node
- we'll eventually need a companion object if we want to increment a counter or do anything else that could be related to a generic state of the node or of the component
- if we have no reference, we won't ever be able to "*unsubscribe*" later on

To solve the first two points of the above list of inefficiencies, the community came up with an idea: the creation of functions on-demand whose context is statically trapped.

```javascript
// utility example
function bindTheContext(fn, context) {
  // return a function that uses a `context` variable
  return function () {
    // and explicitly force fn to use
    // that initial context each time
    return fn.apply(context, arguments);
  };
}

// it just returns the context
function whoIsIt() { return this; }

// both functions are used in the following page
```

```
var me = {name: 'Andrea'}

var alwaysMe = bindTheContext(whoIsIt, me);
// the context `me` is now "trapped" forever
// whenever `alwaysMe()` is invoked

alwaysMe() === me;                    // true → it's always me
alwaysMe.call({}) === me;             // true → it's always me
alwaysMe.call(document) === me;  // true → yet always me!
```

function bind

After being widely adopted, the *"function executed with a trapped context"* pattern became standard, and so the `Function.prototype.bind` was born.

It also uses partial arguments.

```
function sum(x, y) {
   return x + y;
}

// it creates a "function"
// that every time it's invoked
// will use null as execution context
// and the number 5 as its first received argument
var sum5to = sum.bind(null, 5);

console.log(
   sum5to(7),           // 12 → 5+7
   sum5to(1),           // 6  → 5+1
   sum5To(0),           // 5  → 5+0
   sum5To(10, 20)       // 15 → 5+10 (20 ignored)
);
```

Thanks to this method, now we have the ability to reproduce the `ClickCounter` class.

```js
function ClickCounter(el) {
  // the instance inherits these two methods so that
  // we can make their own methods,
  // trapping the instance itself once…
  this.increment = this.increment.bind(this);
  this.stopListening = this.stopListening.bind(this);
  // … that gives us the ability to register
  // these methods and later on to be able
  // to remove them at any time
  el.addEventListener('click', this.increment);
  el.addEventListener(this.drop, this.stopListening);
}

ClickCounter.prototype = {
  drop: 'drop:click-counter',
  value: 0,
  // specific method to increment
  increment: function (evt) {
    // this one will be the trapped
    evt.currentTarget.textContent = ++this.value;
  },
  stopListening: function (evt) {
    var el = evt.currentTarget;
    // we can unsubscribe both methods
    el.removeEventListener('click', this.increment);
    el.removeEventListener(
      this.drop, this.stopListening
    );
  }
};

// here is a new ClickCounter instance
// that shows clicks on the body
new ClickCounter(document.body);
```

Remember: to unsubscribe from an event, you must pass the exact same reference.

Event

Since the beginning of its time, JavaScript has demonstrated its strength and capabilities as an excellent event-driven programming environment.

You can register any sort of event type, and pass around any sort of data, in both browser and server-side engines.

However, the implementation of node.js, an environment that lets you run JavaScript-based programs entirely on the server-side, differs in many ways from the one in the browser.

browser events

Already introduced in the previous pages, browser events can be split into two major categories:

- **user** or **system** events
- **custom** events, also known as *"synthetic"*, which are events generated via code.

When you surf the Web and type on your keyword, click with the mouse, touch the screen with a finger, or use a generic pen pointer, you are creating and implicitly dispatching user events that are specially trusted as user intent.

`mousemove`, `touchstart`, `keypress`, `input`, `load`, `focus` and `blur` are only few of the dozens of well known events available in every browser by default. If you search for *"DOM events"* in *Wikipedia*, there's quite a good list of most of the best-known events.

bubbling and capturing

It should be now clear that the DOM contains trees. A peculiarity of each tree is the possibility to reach into each branch, a procedure also described as *DOM tree traversing*.

By default, every event does this traversing, starting from the `document`, reaching the node that was the *event target*, and bubbling up again.

```
// per each element of this Array …
[
  document,
  document.documentElement,
  document.body
].forEach(function(el) {
  // add the same event type …
  el.addEventListener(this.type, this, true);
  //                  true for capturing ↑
  el.addEventListener(this.type, this, false);
  //                  false for bubbling ↑
  //                  false is also the default
}, {
  type: 'click',                // the event type
  handleEvent: function (e) {   // the listener
    console.log(
      e.currentTarget.nodeName, // where the listener
                                // was added via forEach

      e.target.nodeName,    // the node that created
                            // this event notification
      e.eventPhase === e.CAPTURING_PHASE
    );
  }
});
```

The `e.CAPTURING_PHASE` constant is actually inherited from the `Event` constructor.

This is one of the differences between the classes in JavaScript, and the classes in the DOM.

The `document.documentElement` is the always available HTML root of all node.

To better understand what we are doing, now it's probably a good time to switch to an empty page.

It is usually possible to do this by simply typing `about:blank` in the URL bar, which is the one where we usually write the website address such as *www...*, the one we could use to do a search.

If you open the console and write the previous `forEach` code in there, once you press enter and click on any available white space on the page, you should see the following:

```
#document  BODY  true    // it starts capturing
                         // from the document
HTML      BODY  true     // it traverses the HTML node
                         // to reach the target
BODY      BODY  false    // it reaches the target,
                         // nothing to capture anymore
BODY      BODY  false    // it starts bubbling up
                         // from the target
HTML      BODY  false    // so it will trigger
                         // the parent HTML node listener
#document  BODY  false   // until bubbling reaches
                         // the document listener
```

Again, here is what happens in the capturing phase: document → html → body

And here is what happens in the bubbling: body → html → document

event.stopPropagation()

Traversing can be expensive, especially when in huge nested trees. If a specific listener has no meaning for other nodes, stopPropagation can interrupt the event bubbling or capturing phase, dropping the current event's propagation.

Take the previous example with click listener. Simply adding e.stopPropagation(), at the beginning of the handleEvent method, never lets the click reach other nodes.

```
#document  BODY  true  // e.stopPropagation()
                       // on document capturing phase
```

The line above is all you are going to see in the console. The target, which is the document.body, never sees the event coming. The same happens, if we stop the event propagation during a bubbling phase. Once it reaches the event.target, it won't bubble up anymore.

```
body        → html     → document   // BUBBLING
document    → html     → body       // CAPTURING

              evt.stopPropagation();
body        →|                       // stop BUBBLING
document    →|                       // stop CAPTURING
```

event.preventDefault()

If a node has some special action associated to it, the `.preventDefault()` method prevents that action from happening. Are you clicking on a link? Preventing the default won't let the browser follow that link! Are you filling out some form? Preventing the default won't let you change the text in the input or it won't let you submit that form.

```
function justPreventDefault(e) { e.preventDefault(); }

// it won't open the link
a.addEventListener('click', justPreventDefault);

// it won't let you write in `input`
input.addEventListener('keydown', justPreventDefault);
```

With the touch events, you can even prevent pages from scrolling!

CustomEvent

Whenever we want to create our own synthetic events, the DOM provides its own constructor which Web IDL describes as follows:

```
[
  // new CustomEvent('event-type', {detail: anyValue})
  Constructor(
    DOMString type,
    optional CustomEventInit eventInitDict
  ),
  // available on pages and web workers
  Exposed=(Window, Worker)
]
  // implements Event interface
  interface CustomEvent : Event {
    // the main difference with regular events
    readonly attribute any detail;
  };

// it describes the CustomEventInit object
// expected as an option
dictionary CustomEventInit : EventInit {
  // by default, detail property will be null
  any detail = null;
};
```

Well, maybe the Web IDL format is a bit lengthy, but it surely provides all necessary details.

```
// TL;DR (Too Long, Didn't Read)
var myEvent = new CustomEvent('my:type', {detail: {
  any: 'sort',
  of: 'data',
  iCould: function () {
    return 'possibly think about';
  }
}});

// so that if we have such listener in some node
document.addEventListener(
  'my:type',
  function onMyType(evt) {
    console.log(
      evt.type,
      evt.detail,
      evt.detail.iCould()
    );
  }
);

// we can dispatch the event,
// invoking the associated listener
document.dispatchEvent(myEvent);
```

Since the `CustomEvent` interface also implements the generic `Event`, each previously described method, such as `evt.preventDefault()`, `evt.stopPropagation()`, and the `currentTarget` property will be available, making the event look *"real"*.

EventEmitter

When it comes to server-side events, taking node.js as the main example, the entire capturing and bubbling story doesn't make sense anymore: there is no tree to consider there, just a possible amount of listeners ready to react to asynchronously emitted events.

The type of received arguments is also very different, and the most commonly used *"signature"* for listeners is the `function (possibleError, possibleReturn) {}` one.

signature

In JS and in programming in general, a function signature refers to the whole description of the generic function: its name, the names of all expected parameters, the scope in which the function always executes, and other possibly relevant info about it.

```
// the function sum accepts two arguments,
// and returns their sum
var sum = function (a, b) { return a + b; };
// the function mul also accepts two arguments
// but it does something else
var mul = function (a, b) { return a * b; };
```

In short, both `sum` and `mul` functions above have the same signature.

parameters

When we define the name and the amount of possible arguments that any developer can pass when invoking a function, we are actually defining the *"function parameters"*.

The reason why we talk about `arguments` instead, is that this reference exists and gets created every time a function is invoked, making the relation easier to understand.

node.js events

Events are provided by objects that expose a mechanism to register and eventually remove them. To create objects that are able to emit events, we need the events module.

```
// a CommonJS module example
var events = require('events');
// which exports EventEmitter
var EventEmitter = events.EventEmitter;
// which is a constructor
var nodeEventTarget = new EventEmitter;

nodeEventTarget.on('an-event', function (err, data) {
  //      common node.js callback signature ↑       ↑
  if (err) {
    console.error('something terrible happened', err);
  } else {
    console.log('Data received!', data);
  }
});

// let's try a successful notification
nodeEventTarget.emit('an-event', null, {some:'data'});
// now let's try a failing notification
nodeEventTarget.emit('an-event', new Error('Oh Dear!'));
```

While `obj.on(type, listener)` is a shortcut to `obj.addListener(type, listener)`, there is no `obj.off` method but a `obj.removeListener(type, listener)` one.

🔎 The `EventEmitter` class historically accept only functions as listeners, no objects and therefore no `handleEvent`.

WeakMap

Every time you add a listener to an object that acts like an `EventTarget`, you are basically creating some sort of *"invisible relation"* between those two objects.

As an example, if we don't have a reference to a generic listener, we cannot possibly remove it from the node, or the object, which we used to subscribe for a specific event.

At the same time, that same object does not expose a mechanism to reach any of its subscribers.

Back to the listener object example, whenever you perform the following operation:

```
node.addEventListener(
  'event-name',
  {handleEvent: function (e) {}}
);
```

you tell the browser to somehow link the fresh new listener object to that node.

However, if you remove the node from the document, so that it becomes unreachable and it can be removed from the memory, its object listener also disappears from the memory.

This kind of relationship between objects is called *"weak"*, and it can be manually created.

```
// create a weak map instance
var wm = new WeakMap;

// relate a generic object
function weakData(obj) {
  // which if not in the `wm` instance
  if (!wm.has(obj)) {
    // will link it with `{}` as a value
    wm.set(obj, {});
  }
  // returns the associated link
  return wm.get(obj);
}

// it could be any kind of object
var myReference = {};

// add a property
weakData(myReference).relationship = 'ninja';

console.log(
  // the object is unaffected
  myReference.relationship,
  // the weakly referenced is
  weakData(myReference).relationship
);
```

Symbol

Mentioned as *type* right at the beginning of this glossary, symbols are special keys used to set or read uniquely identified object properties. They can be useful to avoid name clashes.

```
var obj = {};
// create a key named "unique"
var uniqueKey = Symbol('unique');
obj[uniqueKey] = 123;
// create another key named "unique"
var anotherKey = Symbol('unique');
console.log(
  obj[uniqueKey],  // 123
  obj[anotherKey]  // undefined, it's a unique key!
);
```

A peculiarity of `Symbol` is that it cannot be created as `new Symbol()` or it will throw an error. *"... but why?"* Because `typeof Symbol() === "symbol"` which is consistent with the way constructors create other *primitives* such as `"string"`, `"boolean"`, or `"number"`.

The following is a common expectation problem with JavaScript *primitives* created via `new`:

```
typeof new String('');  // "object" which is wrong
                        // if one expect "string"
typeof String('');      // "string" which is usually
                        // correct/expected
```

primitives

Any value where `typeof` returns something other than `"function"` or `"object"` (and the value is not null) is primitive. The main characteristic of primitives is that it is not possible to attach properties to them: these are all immutable values.

```
var t = true;      t.key = 'value';  // no error,
                                     // but also no value
var s = 'string';  s.key = 'value';  // same as above
var i = 0;         i.key = 'value';  // again …
var k = Symbol();  k.key = 'value';  // … and again

// all things are undefined
console.log(t.key, s.key, i.key, k.key);
```

91

Object.getOwnPropertySymbols(obj) → arrayOfSymbols

The default symbols descriptor is *configurable*, *enumerable*, *writable*, and with a generic *value*, like any other property. However, symbols are "*invisible*" for common operations such as `for/in` loops, `Object.keys(obj)` or `Object.getOwnpropertyNames(obj)`.

```
var obj = {};
var key = Symbol();
obj[key] = 'value'; // symbol assigned like a property

for(var k in obj) console.log(k); // nothing is logged

console.log(
  Object.keys(obj),                 // [] → empty Array
  Object.getOwnPropertyNames(obj),  // [] → empty Array
  Object.getOwnPropertySymbols(obj),// [Symbol()] Array
  key in obj                        // true
  // the `in` operator works with symbols
);
```

It is important to remember that even if they are less "*in your way*", **symbols are not private**. One should also keep in mind that they are just like properties: if the intention is to create an unobtrusive relation between two objects, we are still better off with a new *WeakMap*.

shared Symbols

It's possible to handle globally shared symbols via the `.for(key)` and the `.keyFor(sym)` methods.

```
// grab the global context
var root = this.window || global;
// create 'my:info' labeled symbol
var myKey = Symbol.for('my:info');
// only if not already available
// assign a random value
root[myKey] = Math.random();

console.log(
  Symbol.keyFor(myKey),          // the label 'my:info'
  root[myKey],                   // the random value
  root[Symbol.for('my:info')]    // same as root[myKey]
);
```

special Symbols

The `Symbol` primitive constructor has a few public static properties that are also well known symbols. These properties can be used to change the default way in which our code works. As an example, the `Symbol.iterator`, often aliased as `@@iterator`, can be used to describe how a `for/of` loop would iterate over a generic collection.

for/of loop

In modern JS engines it is possible to iterate over a few collections using `for/of`.

```
for (var value of ['a', 'b', 'c'])
  console.log(value);   // 'a', 'b', 'c'
```

This is possible thanks to the `Symbol.iterator` *"protocol"*, a term used to indicate a specification on how the iterator property should look like, and what it should return.

```
// guess who is it again?
var me = {name: 'Andrea', age: 37};

// define iterator protocol
me[Symbol.iterator] = function () {
  // grab all current keys
  var keys = Object.keys(this), i = 0;
  // return an object ...
  return {
    // with a next method, using
    // a fat arrow syntax to bind `this`,
    // that every time is invoked
    next: () => {
      // return another object with two properties
      return {
        // done → false until the end
        done: keys.length <= i,
        // value → like me[currentKey]
        value: this[keys[i++]]
      };
    }
  };
};
// we can now grab all values 'Andrea', 37
for (var value of me) console.log(value);
```

fat arrow

Modern JavaScript comes with many syntax shortcuts, and fat arrow is probably one of the most useful one. It doesn't need the word `function` to be defined, and it makes `this` and `arguments` references available directly from the outer execution context:

```
function newJS() {
  return () => this;
}
function oldJS() {
  return function () { return this; }.bind(this);
  //                                  ↑ explicit bind
}

var obj = {};
var njs = newJS.call(obj);
var ojs = oldJS.call(obj);

// both return `obj` as explicit context
console.log(njs() === ojs()); // true
```

The syntax can be used as a generic function such as

```
var sum = (a, b) => a + b;
sum(2, 3);              // 5
```

Or it can have a proper function body whenever curly brackets are used.

```
var cube = (num) => {
  num = Math.pow(num, 3);
  return num;
};

console.log(cube(3)); // 27 → (3 * 3 * 3)
```

generator

Let's consider the previously described `Symbol.iterator` protocol again. Having an object that through its `.next()` method invocation returns a new object with `done` and `value` as its properties is common in various parts of the latest language specifications. Generators are another example. A `GeneratorFunction` is defined as a function with a wildcard `*`.

```
// this is a regular function
function regular(a, b, c) { return; }

// while this is a generator
function* generator(a, b, c) { return; }
//         ↑ and suddenly ... the wildcard appears
```

Contrary to functions, generators do not execute once invoked, they create some sort of *"magic"* scope that is paused by default and it won't move on unless one asks for it.

```
function* playList(groups) {// #1 paused
  return groups.length;     // #2 ended
}
// nothing happens ... we are paused at point #1
var music = playList([
  'Pearl Jam', 'Foo Fighters', 'Tool'
]);

// to reach the generator returned value ...
var result = music.next();  // move on until the end
console.log(result);        // {done: true, value: 3}
```

The previously mentioned paused execution refers to the generator and the generator only, resulting in a *non-blocking* piece of code. It's possible to decide when a generator should pause at any time, using the special `yield` keyword.

yield

Similarly to a mp3 player's pause button, every `yield` pauses a generator execution.

```
function* playList(groups) {  // #1
  var i = 0;
  // until we have listened to all groups
  while (i < groups.length) {
    // use groups[i] as value and pause
    yield groups[i++];
  }
  return 'listened to ' + i + ' groups';
}

var music = playList(['Pearl Jam', 'Tool']);
// playing music in 3 ... 2 ... 1 ...
```

```js
// let's listen to one group at a time
console.log(music.next());
// {done: false, value: 'Pearl Jam'}

// let's have a break, music is paused,
// can we do something else?
console.log('is this console responsive?'); // it is!

// ok, the music is on again, who was next?
console.log(music.next());
// {done: false, value: 'Tool'}

// awesome!!! any other group to listen to?
console.log(music.next());
// {done: true, value: 'listened to 2 groups'}
```

When the `while` loop condition isn't satisfied anymore, there is no other `yield` to pause the music execution. This flags the iteration as `done`, where the `value` is optionally the returned one, in this example that is simply the number of groups that were played.

You can always generate a new `playList` with other groups and listen to them.

```js
var rock = playList(
  ['Foo Fighters', 'Pearl Jam', 'Tool']
);
var classic = playList(
  ['L. van Beethoven', 'W.A. Mozart', 'A. Vivaldi']
);

rock.next();     // after this I feel like classic …
classic.next();  // d'you know what? rock again!
rock.next();     //   \,,/(>.<)\,,/
```

generator.next(value) → {done:boolean, value:any}

In previous examples we have only checked what kind of object `gen.next()` returned.

However, that's not the only trick as it can also send a value.

```
// its internal while loop will never exit
function* forever() {
  // an integer to increment per each while
  var sent = 0;
  // it's safe because generators can pause
  while (true) {
    var received = yield sent++;
    //                  ↑ sent will be the value
    //                    of the object returned
    //                    when we'll invoke
    //                    gen.next() the first time
    console.log(received);
    //            ↑ will log the value in gen.next(value)
  }
}
```

It is important to remember that `yield` pauses *"right to left"*, that is it sends out its optional right hand value, and it eventually assigns to its left hand the `gen.next(one)`.

This explains why the very first time we call `.next()` we cannot pass in any value: we simply start the execution of the function, until we stop and receive the very first yielded value, if any.

Below there is an example that will miss the very first value passed along.

```
// g is now paused on top of forever
var g = forever();

// first yield is 0, 'A' is ignored
console.log(g.next('A').value);
// 'B' received, while loop will yield → 2
console.log(g.next('B').value);
// 'C' received, while loop will yield → 3
console.log(g.next('C').value);
```

Following an attempt to describe what happens while we loop.

```
function* forever() {        g.next('A')
    var sent = 0;
    while (true) {
        var received =
                        yield sent++;  → {value: 0}
                                            g.next('B')

                                        → {value: 1}
    }                                       g.next('C')
}
```

generator.throw(error)

If something goes wrong during an iteration, it is possible to exit from the generator either by returning, as in a regular function, or by throwing an error. The whole point of having generators though, is the ability to control them from the outside without direct access to their scope or context, but with the equivalent of the remote control *"play/pause"* buttons.

The `gen.throw(new Error('get out!'))` method gives us the ability to also force the generator to stop its execution, even if nothing wrong happened in its execution scope.

Promises

If we need to chain a sequence of asynchronous operations we have a few options:

- nest callbacks if scoped references are relevant
- pass dozens of relevant references to each function needed in the process
- attach any sort of data at runtime and invoke bound methods all over

However, if we want to handle possible errors during this process we are basically doomed, so this is the moment when a `Promise` could save the day.

Asynchronous approach
```
async(input, (out) => {
  // use output +
  // do something else
}
```

Promise-based approach
```
promise(input).then((out)=>{
  // use output +
  // return some value
}
```

There is a subtle but very relevant difference between the classic and Promise-based approach which is that a `Promise` instance can be passed around as it is, and we can then add our logic at any time by simply invoking its `.then(callback)` method.

```
var waitTillThisBookIsFinished = new Promise(
// a new Promise requires a function
// which will be invoked later on
// once this function is invoked
// it will receive two arguments:
function (
  resolve,  // a resolved function to invoke
            // once we our business is done
  rejected  // a rejected function to invoke
            // in case something goes wrong
) {
  var thingsToWrite = 1000; // a thousand things to write
  var bookContent = '';      // from no content
  while (thingsToWrite--) { // to "All The Things"!
    bookContent += 'moOAR content';
  }
  // the book is finished and resolved
  resolve(bookContent);
});

// whoever is waiting for it could read its content
waitTillThisBookIsFinished.then(function (content) {
  // once resolved
  console.log(content);
});

// somebody else
waitTillThisBookIsFinished.then(function (content) {
  // and someone else could do something else
  writeARantAboutTheBook(content);
});
```

Promises are best used with asynchronous code.

The example above is only a walk through the logic involved and not a best practice.

"One shot" asynchronous operations are indeed the best kind to be solved with Promises.

```js
var userAskedToIgnoreTheApp = new Promise(
  function (res, rej) {
    document
      // find the app button to add the listener
      .querySelector('#app-banner button.nope')
      .addEventListener('click', function fn(e) {
        // clean up and resolve once clicked
        e.currentTarget.removeEventListener(e.type, fn);
        res();
      });
  }
);
// whenever that click happens
userAskedToIgnoreTheApp.then(function () {
  localStorage.setItem('dont-bother-again', true);
}); // ↑ it's a little synchronous browser's database
```

promise.then(resolved, rejected) → newPromise

If a promise invokes its received `reject(anyValue)` function, by simply using `.then(notify)` there will be no effects:

there is also the need for a callback for possible errors.

```js
var p = new Promise(function (resolve, reject) {
  reject('because');
});
p.then(
  // will never happen because rejected
  function yep(result) { console.log('All good!'); },
  // 'because' error in console
  function nope(err) { console.error(err); }
);
```

promise.then(resolved).catch(anyError) → newPromise

If an error occurs inside any invokation of the promise chain, only the .catch(function) will be notified, (not the rejected one).

This is actually an important distinction between these two patterns because one really involves a manual rejection, while the other reacts even if the promise has already been resolved.

Following there is an example code.

```
var p = new Promise(function (res, rej) { res('OK'); });
p.then(
  function yep(result) {
    console.log('All good!');         // 'All good!'
    throw new Error('actually no!');  // damn it!
  },
  function nope(err) {
    console.error('nope', err);       // never will
  }
).catch(function (err) {
  console.error('caught', err);       // here we are
});
```

promise.then(fn).then(fn).then(fn) → newPromise

Every time we invoke .then(fn) we create a new promise from the initial chain. The main difference between promises created via a chain and simple promises is that for the ones created via a chain we need to return some value or they won't receive the result.

```
var pRoot = new Promise((res, rej) => res('OK'));
var pFirst = pRoot.then(function (info) {
  console.log(info);   // 'OK'
  return 123;          // pSecond is chaining from pFirst
                       // it will receive 123 as info
});
var pSecond = pFirst.then(function (info) {
  console.log(info);   // 123
});
```

If we want to expose the received data we can simply return that, otherwise we can return a different result, or even nothing.

Promise.all(arrayOfPromises) → newPromise

Asynchronous non-blocking operations are not necessarily related to each other.

Think about organizing a vacation, one has to think about transport tickets, booking a hotel, renting a car, and finally preparing some luggage.

```
// planning a vacation through an Array of Promises
Promise.all([
  new Promise(function (res, rej) {
    res('hotel booked!');      // book a room
  }),
  new Promise(function (res, rej) {
    res('flight booked!');     // book the flight
  }),
  new Promise(function (res, rej) {
    res('luggage ready!');     // prepare the luggage
  }),
  new Promise(function (res, rej) {
    res('car rented!');        // rent a car
  })
]).then(function (results) {
  console.log(results);        // awesome, we can GO!!!
  // ["hotel booked!", "flight booked!",
  //  "luggage ready!", "car rented!"]
});
```

Whenever any of those Promises fail, the rejected catcher will know, and we will probably have to reschedule our entire vacation. Let's hope not!

Promise.resolve(value) → newPromise

If we'd like to create a promise that is already resolved, `Promise.resolve(value)` is a handy shortcut. Its counter part is `Promise.reject(anyValue)` which provides a similar counter utility.

```
var p = Promise.resolve('any value');
p.then(function (result) { console.log(result); });
```

Generators and Promises

Let's have a look at the following utility, originally explained in promisejs.org: it combines both patterns.

```javascript
// syncLike accepts a generator function
function syncLike(genFunc) {
  // and it returns an anonymous function
  return function () {
    // that once invoked
    var
      // will create a generator
      gen = genFunc.apply(this, arguments),
      // and it will manage it here
      handle = (result) => {
        // it will return a Promise,
        // no matter what the value is
        var p = Promise.resolve(result.value);
        // if the generator hasn't finished yet, we can
        // chain a new Promise passing
        // `next` and `orFail` as callbacks
        return result.done ? p : p.then(next, orFail);
      },
      next   = (value) => handle(gen.next(value)),
      orFail = (error) => handle(gen.throw(error))
    ;          // `next` and `orFail` return ↑ promises
               // chained via `handle`
    // our journey begins starting the generator
    try { return next(null); }
    // and with a fallback in case something fails
    catch(err) { return Promise.reject(err);}
    // it's a Promise "circus" that drives a generator
  };
}
```

It's hard to understand what's going on until we see a concrete example so here it is:

do you remember when we talked about planning your vacation? Following how it could look like now:

```js
// it returns a new Promise that will resolve
function arrange(what) {
  return new Promise(res => res(what + ' is ready'));
}
// an always welcomed activity to do ^_^;
var letsGoOnVacation = syncLike(function* () {
  // multiple var declaration
  var
    // it will arrange the Hotel
    hotel = yield arrange('hotel'),
    // it will arrange the flight
    flight = yield arrange('flight'),
    // it will arrange the luggage
    luggage = yield arrange('luggage'),
    // it will arrange the car too
    car = yield arrange('car')
  ;
  console.log("let's go!", hotel, flight, luggage, car);
});
letsGoOnVacation(); // it will log everything:
// let's go! The hotel, the flight, the luggage,
// and the car are ready!
```

Using promises to somehow resolve generators is a nice way to make the code look synchronous.

If you are wondering whether `Promise.all` could have been used instead of having to wait for one action after the other one, the answer is Yes!

And that would have been more efficient, for the simple reason that we could have executed all those actions in parallel.

```js
// a better approach to multiple asynchronous actions
var letsGoOnVacation = syncLike(function* () {
  console.log("let's go!", yield Promise.all([
    arrange('hotel'),
    arrange('flight'),
    arrange('luggage'),
    arrange('car')
  ]));
});
```

To conclude: Promises' main strength, but also their main caveat, is the fact that they cannot be cancelled.

That means that we might regret using them for any operation that could take a long time, as these are probably the wrong solution to the problem. Instead we could track those through a progress-friendly operation, something a file download or an image upload could require.

Timers

Asynchronous code have been already mentioned, but so far without concretely testing what they are about. Well, asynchronous is not usually something created just for fun, but rather an inevitable part of our application, such as a database query, a client/server interaction, a worker notification, and so on.

JavaScript also offers its own mechanisms to schedule the execution of some arbitrary code at some point in time. The most documented and widely implemented functions to schedule such executions are `setTimeout` and `setInterval`, which are both capable of detaching from the current execution flow in a non-blocking way.

setTimeout(fn, delay, arg1, arg2, argN) → timerIdentifier

To schedule the invocation of any function at any time in the future and once, `setTimeout` is the way.

```
// scheduling to be executed in 1 second
var t = setTimeout(
  // it will receive arguments, if specified
  function laterOn(logMe) {
    console.log(logMe);
  },
  // it's the delay represented in milliseconds
  1000,
  // it's the optional `logMe` argument passed later on
  Math.random()
);
```

If you are patient enough to wait for a whole second, you'll see the random number returned by `Math.random()` invocation appear in the console. However, if you are no longer interested in that operation, you can always clean it up, as long as you hold its identifier.

clearTimeout(timerIdentifier)

If you set a timer, you should be able to cancel it too. This method does exactly that.

```
var ti = setTimeout(console.log, 1000, 'content');
clearTimeout(ti); // print will not be invoked
```

setInterval(fn, delay, arg1, arg2, argN) → timerIdentifier

If `setTimeout` schedules the function to be executed once, `setInterval` schedules it to be executed every `delay` milliseconds.

```
// every 1 millisecond!
var chronograph = setInterval(
  // invoke this function
  function (startTime, nDigits) {
    // check time difference
    var time = new Date(Date.now() - startTime);
    console.log([
      //         log  HH hours
      nDigits(2, time.getHours()),
      //         with MM minutes
      nDigits(2, time.getMinutes()),
      //         and  SS seconds
      nDigits(2, time.getSeconds()),
      //         plus mmm milliseconds
      nDigits(3, time.getMilliseconds())
    ].join(':'));
  },
  1,          // try each millisecond
  Date.now(), // using this  startTime
  // and using this function which converts
  // 1s to '01' or 1ms to '001'
  (n, i) => (Array(n).join('0') + i).slice(-n)
);
```

When starting the above chronograph, a pretty fast list of logs will show how much time elapsed since its beginning. We can stare at it, or stop it!

clearInterval(timerIdentifier)

It has the exact same logic and behavior as seen for the `clearTimeout`. If you want to stop an interval:

```
clearInterval(chronograph);// stops logging elapsed time
```

And that's it folks, no more frenetic logs in our console. There is one caveat about timers and that is their scheduled execution. If we set a timeout at a second, but at some point there's a long operation that takes 2 seconds, our timer cannot invoke the scheduled callback before the 2 seconds or longer. The same goes for the interval: if we schedule anything under 10 ms, the timer will try to execute too much, and will keep queuing invokes to the possibly already delayed execution queue. For instance, in the previous chronograph the timer was scheduled at 1 ms, but the console didn't show every single ms, each was resolved as soon as possible, but never sooner than 4 to 10 milliseconds or more.

requestAnimationFrame(fn) → rafIdentifier

In the DOM *User Interface (UI)* world, when it comes to update any visible information on the page, there is a need for a better scheduler than timers and *"rAF"* was indeed born for that.

```
// optionally needed to cancel
var rafIdentifier;
// "rAF" has no extra arguments
(function (startTime, nDigits) {
  // so we IIFE our chronograph
  (function chronograph(diff) {
    var time = new Date(Date.now() - startTime);
    document.body.textContent = [
      nDigits(2, time.getHours()),
      nDigits(2, time.getMinutes()),
      nDigits(2, time.getSeconds()),
      nDigits(3, time.getMilliseconds())
    ].join(':');
    // and we schedule via rAF again
    rafIdentifier = requestAnimationFrame(chronograph);
  }());
}(
  Date.now(),
  (n, i) => (Array(n).join('0') + i).slice(-n)
));
```

Just like with timers, you can clear a *"rAF"* via `cancelAnimationFrame(rafIdentifier)`.

process.nextTick(fn)

Node.js has a way to schedule functions and let them execute ASAP, while keeping the execution queue somehow under control. Whenever you want to avoid blocking the current thread and schedule an async operation, `nextTick` will do it.

requestIdleCallback(fn, waitExpiresIn) → ricIdentifier

Back to DOM, there is the possibility to schedule callbacks when the browser is less busy, and this is the case for *"rIC"*.

```
// it was created to schedule less important tasks
requestIdleCallback(
  function justChecking() {
    console.log('just checking if everything is fine');
    // reschedule if necessary
    requestIdleCallback(justChecking, 2000);
  },
  2000   // ← wait max 2 seconds then
         //   execute this task if not already run
);
```

Remember: apart from Promises, every other asynchronous operation can be cancelled, and *"rIC"* is no exception. Use `cancelIdleCallback(ricIdentifier)` and you are done.

template strings

We have covered so much but we still don't know much about strings, and even less about templates.

First of all, strings can be concatenated via the + operator, or using the method `.concat(one[, orMore])` inherited from the `String.prototype`.

```
// concatenating via +
var a = 'this ' + 'is ' + 1 + ' string!';
// str.concat(a, b, c)
var b = 'this '.concat('is ', 1, ' string!');
console.log(a, b); // it logs the same string twice
```

108

Neither single nor double-quoted strings support multiple lines.

Moreover, if one wants to include a dynamic value in a string, they have to close the quote, concatenate the reference, and eventually open other quotes again.

Single or double quoted

```
function greetings(who) {
  return 'Hello ' + who +
  ',\n  thank you' +
  ' for being here!';
}
```

Template strings

```
function greetings(who) {
  return `Hello ${name}
  thank you for being here!
  `;
}
```

The above comparison shows the difference between quotes and backticks: with latter we can not only forget about new line problems, but we can also access local references, including `this` context.

The syntax is represented by the delimiters `${ }` within which we could write JS.

tagged template strings

A special power of back-ticked strings is their *"tag-ability"*. A tag is a function that will be executed receiving an array of strings found right before and after possible curly brackets as first argument, and zero, one or more computed values as a result of whatever code is present inside those possible curly brackets found in the string.

```
function tagLogger(
  statics // first argument is always an Array
) {
  // if there are extra arguments
  for (var i = 1; i < arguments.length; i++) {
    console.log(statics[i - 1]);    // log previous text
    console.log(arguments[i]);       // log current value
  }
  console.log(statics[i - 1]);       // log last string
}
// we can tag any "backticked" string now
// and check the console → 'before ', 5, ' after'
tagLogger `before ${2 + 3} after`;
```

Tag functions are especially handy when it comes to transforming values before returning them.

```js
function htmlAttributes(markup) {
  for (var
    // declares an output
    out = [],
    // a regular expression
    re = /[&<>'"]/g,
    // and a transformer
    fn = (m) => ('&#'+m.charCodeAt(0)+';'),
    i = 1; i < arguments.length; i++
  ) {
    out.push(
      markup[i - 1],
      arguments[i].replace(re, fn)
    );
  }
  out.push(markup[i - 1]);
  return out.join('');   // transformed
}
var value = '<any"thing>';
console.log(
  // evil input sanitized
  htmlAttributes `<input value="${value}">`
);
// <input value="&#60;any&#34;thing&#62;">
```

regular expression

The `RegExp` constructor, together with its instances, brings in a powerful syntax that is capable of searching, matching, testing, or replacing strings through special letters with special meanings.

There are many caveats, possible security implications, string encoding issues, and modern or older ways to deal with them that I don't think it'd be wise to partially cover them in here.

What is important to know is their literal syntax representation:

```
// how to recognize a literal, inline, RegExp instance
var regExp = /^(?:search)*via.[specia-l]chars/gim;
//            ▲ begins                      ends ▲ ▲
//            └──────────────────────────────────┘ │
//                         optional g,i,m,u flags ─┘
```

JSON

A JS glossary without an explanation about the *"JavaScript Object Notation"* would not be credible, so here it is:

JSON is the string representation standard for objects, arrays, strings, booleans, numbers, null and nothing else.

```
// JSON can represent as string the following values
var obj = {JSON:["string",1.2,{},[],true,false,null]};
var str = JSON.stringify(obj);
// '{"JSON":["string",1.2,{},[],true,false,null]}'
```

We can parse a string via `JSON.parse(str)` or encode any compatible value using `JSON.stringify(compatibleValue)` and both methods would accept a callback as an option.

The callback will be invoked while reading each entry or while reviving values during parsing.

Math

This globally available object is full of methods whose aim is to help us doing ... math!

The most commonly used are `Math.pow(num, power)`, `Math.sqrt(num, radix)`, `Math.max(num1, num2, numN)` and `Math.min(num1, num2, numN)`, but you can always check all of them by name, and eventually investigate their signature online.

```
// the following is a generic helper
// that tells us a lot about any object
function tellMeAbout(that) {
  console.log(Object.getOwnPropertyNames(that));
}
tellMeAbout(Math);   // let's see what's in there!
```

parseInt(string, base) → integerNumber

Whenever you deal with user input, you deal with strings. If you ask for the age or any other integer number, `parseInt` will help you transform the user input.

```
console.log(
  // we can avoid specifying the base, however
  parseInt('3'),
  parseInt('11', 2),    // 11 in base 2 is 3, not 11
  parseInt('08', 10),   // 08 in an octal base is 0, not 8
  parseInt('FF', 16)    // FF in base 10 would be an error
                        // not hexadecimal for 255
);
```

parseFloat(string) → floatNumber

When you need to transform a string into a floating number, `parseFloat` is the way to go. It doesn't accept any extra argument so a `parseFloat('FF')` would result into a NaN value, because it would not be recognized as a number or hex string.

Recent ECMAScript features

Since I've started writing this glossary, few things changed already in JavaScript. The ECMAScript speicifcation is indeed a living, and rolling, standard. This means that new features becomes available as soon as all staging steps are matched.

There are few modern topics omitted in this glossary but described online and few others worth a quick exploration.

let declaration

A `var` declaration can be defined in any line of a generic function but it's available in the whole body, even if defined after a condition.

```
function hoisted(shouldDefine) {
  console.log(value);   // undefined
  if (shouldDefine) {
    var value = 123;
  }
  return value;
}

hoisted(false);         // undefined
hoisted(true);          // 123
```

The same happens for generic `for` loops.

```
for (var i = 0; i < 1; i++) console.log(i); // 0
console.log(i);                             // 1
```

Modern JavaScript engines can declare block scoped variable through the `let` keyword, being sure such declarations won't interfere with the surrounding code.

```
function hoisted(shouldDefine) {
  if (shouldDefine) {
    let value = 123;
    // this is the only part of the function
    // where accessing `value` won't throw an error
    return value;
  }
}
```

```
for (let i = 0; i < 1; i++) console.log(i); // 0
console.log(i); // throw ReferenceError:i is not defined
```

rest parameters

There are cases a function could accept one or more arguments.

The `rest` feature simplifies eventual boilerplate needed to loop over `arguments`.

```
function sum(a, b, ...others) {
  let c = a + b;
  while (others.length) {
    // returns and drop the value at index 0
    c += others.shift();
  }
  return c;
}

sum(1, 2, 3, 4);  // 10
```

spread operator

Another simplification, this time for the common `.apply(context, arguments)` pattern.

```
var numbers = [1, 7, -3, 4];

// Math.max accepts N values and returns the higher
Math.max.apply(Math, numbers);  // 7
Math.max(...numbers);           // 7
```

Map

Similarly to `WeakMap`, Map instances can relate objects but it's your responsibility to remove such relation.

Set, and WeakSet

Meant to simplify unique collections related operations, Set and WeakSet are similar to Map and WeakMap except the key is internal and their values are always unique.

Proxy

Recently revisited, the `Proxy` constructor has the ability to transparently wrap a generic object and intercept upfront all operations.

```
var object = {};
var proxied = new Proxy(object, {
  has: function (target, prop) {
    return target.hasOwnProperty(prop);
  }
});

'toString' in object;    // true, inherited
'toString' in proxied;   // false, not own property

object.toString = function () { return 'hello proxy'; };
'toString' in proxied;   // true
```

The `in` case is just one of the many possibilities, all described online in the MDN Proxy page.

destructuring

It is possible to declare variables while extracting values from arrays or objects.

```
// destructuring arrays
let [a, b] = ['a', 'b'];   // a === 'a', b === 'b'

// destructuring objects
let {a, b} = {a: 1, b: 2}; // a === 1,   b === 2
```

JavaScript F.A.Q. on demand

Below there is a list of quick answers to the most frequently asked questions:

- **is JavaScript safe?** We can write good and bad code with pretty much every programming language and the more we know about it, the safer it becomes.
- **is JavaScript fast?** Overall yes, and on top of that, there are various efforts from major players to make it as fast as native C or C++ could be.
- **what else should I know about JS?** I've been using JS and its variants for the last 16 years and yet, I still don't know the entire API exposed in every different client or server environment. Every occasion to learn more is a good one, but first you should try to understand if you are interested in frontend or backend development. Also, try to read updated books, because in the last 20 years JS has been changing a lot. It's good to know the past, but at the end of the day we are going to use modern features.
- **have you heard about transpilers?** I have not only heard about them, but I use them, too. For example, most of the agnostic examples in this glossary have been successfully tested via `babel-node`, a command line interface (*CLI*) that brings the latest features from the latest `ECMAScript` specifications to node.js. Would I use them in production? It depends!
- **what does "*in production*" mean?** It's the official version, currently offered to every user, of a generic website, application, framework, design or program. It's what we deliver, as opposite to what we"*prototype*" to quickly test our ideas.
- **what does "*prototype*" mean?** I know this glossary might have been confusing, but when it comes to non-technical JS discussions, a prototype is a sketch, or a quickly created version of a final product, that should probably never go to production as it is.

- **which FrameWork, library or tool should I use?** The one that solves your problem, if any. Otherwise you are better off with what the frontend or backend core already offers.
- **is JavaScript for web pages only?** These days it's hard to find electronics that don't run JS. Smart watches, routers, your current computer, or even colorful led light bulbs, are compatible with some JavaScript engine or are already running it.
- **is JavaScript memory safe?** There is a *Garbage Collector* that takes care of cleaning up the mess we created. What we can do is to help it doing its job, for example by not holding values indefinitely.

There surely are other questions that I've missed here, to which I encourage you to look for answers. A good place with decent, usually up to date documentation is the MDN – Mozilla Developer Network.

There are many other topics I didn't have the chance to talk about, such as: *Web Workers*, *Service Worker*, *IndexedDB*, local and *sessionStorage*, *Ajax* via *XMLHttpRequest* and the recent *Fetch API*, but I believe that if you made it this far, you are now able to understand most online technical articles.

Useful links

Mozilla Developer Network	developer.mozilla.org
World Wide Web Consortium	www.w3.org
WHATWG	whatwg.org
Node.JS	nodejs.org
Babel JS	babeljs.io
YDKJS (book series)	youdontknowjs.com
Exploring ES6	exploringjs.com

www.ingramcontent.com/pod-product-compliance
Lightning Source LLC
Chambersburg PA
CBHW072215170526
45158CB00002BA/609